# THE CORPORATE STATE
# IN ACTION

# THE CORPORATE STATE
# IN ACTION
## *ITALY UNDER FASCISM*

By CARL T. SCHMIDT

Lecturer in Economics at Columbia University

OXFORD UNIVERSITY PRESS

New York   Toronto

1939

DG
571
532

9/16/39   1.97   (Av.) Stech.

18220

TO

GAETANO SALVEMINI

And whereas states consist of two classes, of poor men and of rich, the tyrant should lead both to imagine that they are preserved and prevented from harming one another by his rule, and whichever of the two is stronger he should attach to his government.

Aristotle: *Politics* (Jowett translation)

The cultural effects of the discipline of warfare and armament are much the same whether it is undertaken for dynastic or for business ends; in either case it takes on a dynastic complexion and breeds the temperament, ideals, and institutional habits proper to a dynastic system of politics. The farther it goes the more it comes to make use of business interests as a means rather than an end.

Veblen: *The Theory of Business Enterprise*

# ACKNOWLEDGEMENT

THE Social Science Research Council in 1935 granted me a research fellowship that enabled me to make observations basic to the present study. My obligation to the Council is great. The Columbia University Press kindly permitted me to draw on materials in my study of Italian agricultural policy, *The Plough and the Sword*. I am very grateful to all those whose suggestions aided in the writing of this book.

C.T.S.

*New York City*

# CONTENTS

I. ITALY BEFORE FASCISM                    3

II. THE BLACKSHIRT REVOLUTION              25

III. BUILDING THE POLICE STATE            49

IV. WORKERS OF FIELD AND FACTORY          75

V. BREAD AND LAND                         97

VI. PROPERTY AND PROFITS                  115

VII. THE POWER OF THE SWORD               137

NOTES                                     161

SELECTED BIBLIOGRAPHY                     166

INDEX                                     169

# THE CORPORATE STATE
# IN ACTION

# THE CORPORATE STATE IN ACTION

## I : ITALY BEFORE FASCISM

FIVE hundred years ago the leading thinkers, poets, painters, and engineers of Europe were Italians. Certainly it was not mere coincidence that the leading European business men also were Italians. Genoa, Florence, Milan, Venice, cradled modern business enterprise. In all the arts of profit-making, buying and selling and lending, the Italian merchants were teachers of the English, French, and Germans.

But the great navigations and discoveries of the fifteenth and sixteenth centuries made the Mediterranean an inland sea in a corner of the world. The economic center of Europe shifted to the English Channel. And with it shifted the politically and culturally unifying forces of business enterprise. Thereafter, the Italians slumbered in the evening glories of the Renaissance, dreaming of the material and spiritual grandeur of Roman world empire. The early promise of Italian capitalism was unfulfilled, leaving Italy a land of poor agriculture and localized handicrafts and commerce. As artists of the business traffic, the Northerners soon left the Italians far behind.

The awakened, appraising outsiders saw the hills and valleys beyond the Alps peopled by unlettered yet picturesque peasants and deft, small-scale artisans. They saw these backward regions ruled by a colorful company of petty princes, churchmen, and semi-feudal barons. Here, too, was a battleground for the clashing ambitions of Spanish, French, and Austrian royal dynasties. More than anything else, this was a romantic land of noon-day dreams, of *dolce far niente*. And

Italy, the name itself, was but a convenient geographical expression.

Into this slumbering country rudely broke the revolution of the middle classes of France, led by their advance agent, Napoleon Bonaparte. Napoleon soon disappeared, but the ideas of the revolution remained. The political and economic credo of the middle classes, exalted in the principles of Nationalism and Liberalism, remained to shake the old regime. This it was —expressed in conspiracy, insurrection, and, not least, shrewd diplomacy—that at last welded the little states from the Alps to Sicily into one political whole. Externally, the Italian national upsurge was successful because it served the purposes of major European foreign offices upset by dynastic conflicts. Internally, the *Risorgimento* triumphed because the middle-class credo was embraced by eloquent prophets and intellectuals, armed with sword and pen. Here was a patriotism well suited to the needs of the emerging business community of North Italy, which stood to gain from the wider markets that must come after elimination of internal tariffs and other feudal-mercantilist shackles on commercial enterprise. It was no accident that the King of Piedmont, head of a State already well advanced in modern business affairs, was seated on the throne of the new nation.

As for the underlying populace, the captains and orators were helpful in preaching to it the gospel that whatever is good for the rulers of the united nation is also good for the people. On the whole, however, the lower classes played a passive role in the unification. The great masses of the peasantry were inert, and sometimes even actively resisted the innovations, especially those touching the Church. Yet only a movement of and for the peasants could have given the *Risorgimento* a really popular character. Most 'revolutionaries,' however, shrank back fearfully at the thought of an awakening of the peasantry. Indeed, the specter of social unrest, and a belief that an Italian national monarchy could keep it in check, inspired the benevolence of the foreign offices towards the unification. An Italian historian has said: 'When did the Reaction begin? On the same day as the Revolution.'

Thus United Italy, a creation of the middle-class commercial enterprisers, bureaucrats, and intellectuals, came into being much as did the French and English political nations. Avowedly liberal, it carried on without much benefit of democracy. The State, once the servant of the Prince, became the servant of the new *élite*. But as always before, the underlying masses were expected to identify their own interests with those of their masters, or suffer the consequences.

It was economically a land of many millions of poor peasants and rural laborers, ruled by a few thousand functionaries of the State, intellectuals, landlords, and traders. Four great groups made up the Italian nation: First, the great nobles and the wealthy bourgeoisie, who controlled the large landed estates, banks, and commercial enterprises, and who looked upon the State as essentially their tool. Secondly, the churchmen, whose leaders came from the aristocracy, and whose rank and file were recruited from the peasantry. They stood aloof from the national Government, but were only in small part opposed to the going social order. Thirdly, the lower middle class, comprising the modest landowners, merchants, and traders, and the majority of officials and intellectuals serving as agents of the State. And fourthly, the vast mass of the people, peasants and workers, the unknown Italy, constituting raw material for the policies of the State.

The peasantry—three-quarters of the entire population of Italy—wrested a poor living from the soil. A large proportion of them were dependent workers—that is, wage laborers or crop-sharing tenants. Many peasants, it is true, did own a tiny strip or two planted in wheat, or a row of vines, but they had to earn the rest of their living by working for the bigger landowners. In the main, control of the soil was in hands other than those that cultivated it. As late as the eve of the World War, two-thirds of the farm land belonged to only a quarter of a million proprietors: princes and barons and well-to-do townsmen. The remaining third was divided in small-holdings among nearly five million peasants. And millions of other humble workers were quite landless. Only in parts of Central Italy was there a significant approach to an agriculture of small, relatively prosperous, self-contained farms. The fertile regions of the North were dominated by large-scale, commercial farms, employing much hired labor and more and more adopting mechanical methods. Over great areas of the South the dwarf-holdings of an abjectly poor, town-dwelling peasantry contrasted with huge, almost uninhabited estates, the *latifondi*, used as sheep runs or for primitive cultivation of wheat.

Nor was Italy greatly favored with natural resources. Except for the Po Valley and a few other fertile regions, it was a country of arid hills and mountains, of parched tablelands and swampy moors. Only through the never-ending, back-breaking work of the peasants could Italy's agricultural productivity be maintained. Despite its high human costs, the living of the rural population was meager, often desperately poor. An official enquiry concluded that the living conditions of the Italian peasants and farm workers could hardly have been worse at any time during the previous two thousand years. Wages were a pittance. The wage-working day—when there was such work to be had—lasted from dawn to dusk.

Nor were the share-tenants—bound to give the better part of their crops to the landlords and to do many unpaid chores on the farms and in the landlords' houses—much more fortunate than the wage-workers. The crowded, dirty hovels of the villages, the ravages of malaria, tuberculosis, and pellagra, a shocking illiteracy and superstitition, mirrored the peasants' poverty.

The peasants—that is, most of the people—played no active role in the politics of United Italy. So narrow was the suffrage at first that only two per cent of the population could make even the gesture of electing parliamentary representatives. After the electoral reform of 1882 the great bulk of the people was still without the franchise; not until 1912 was universal male suffrage granted. Occasionally the passivity of the peasants did give way to sudden, blindly violent uprisings against the insolence of tax-collectors and mayors. But these outbursts were as quickly put down by police and soldiers.

The merchants and industrialists, largely concentrated in the North, were not numerous. As their economic power grew, however, the old bureaucratic and landowning aristocracy were obliged to share the political rule with them. But there was no unbridgeable chasm between the ambitions of landlords and business enterprisers. Instead, personal and financial alliances between the two groups soon fused them into a community of interests, operating at the cost of popular well-being. And the chief business of the Government was to protect and promote the interests of the propertied.

The social evils of this fusion were nowhere clearer than in South Italy, in the regions of the old Papal States and the Kingdom of the Two Sicilies. There the old order of absentee landownership continued to rule. The peasants remained as before, the hungry and uninstructed servants of their betters. The illiteracy of the peasantry and insignificance of the lower middle class enabled the aristocratic landlords to have their way politically. And the landlords could be tolerant towards a policy of tariff protection for the industries of the North. Did they not obtain tariff protection for their wheat? They could afford to let the South become virtually a colony of North Italy. It was the workers and peasants, and especially those of the South, who bore the burdens of tariffs and taxes. Well-meaning intellectuals frequently urged that the Government do something toward raising the living levels of the South. But nothing of importance could be achieved unless the dominance of landed and industrial proprietors were broken. Therefore nothing was done.

The professional politicians sought to gloss over this funda-mental cleavage in the nation by means of guile, compromise, and corruption. But there was little hesitation in using the disciplinary measures of bayonet and cannon when they seemed most expedient. The political struggle involved, not parties with broad and definite policies, but opportunistic personal and provincial groups. The powers and pleasures of office passed from one manipulator to another. But the under-lying system of politics, based on a network of local chieftains supplying the necessary votes, did not change. The adminis-trative work of government was the business of a few special-ists and experts, and the political machinery was the private possession of a few 'strong men,' the party dictators. It was said: 'The leader of the orchestra may change, but the music is always the same.' Attainment of office was enough to make the occasional radical into a docile servant of the Crown. A tradition of genuine parliamentary government could hardly take root among the people. And doubts about the real worth of parliamentarism were nurtured among the intellectual onlookers.

Another source of weakness for the new regime was its conflict with the Roman Church. Before unification, the Papacy ruled not only a world-wide Church, but also a substantial part of Italy. Indeed, to nationally-minded people the Pope was, more than anything else, an Italian petty prince wearing priestly garments. As such, he stood in the way of Italian political unity. But with the progress of nationalism, culminating in the entry of the Piedmontese King into Rome, the Papacy lost its temporal powers. The Pope shut himself in the Vatican, and there railed against the usurpers. Secretly, and at times almost openly, the Papacy worked in the European diplomatic offices for a foreign intervention that would restore its old Italian domination. During the '70s and '80s the Great Powers, in turn, found the 'Roman Question' convenient as a lever with which to bend Italian policy to their interests. Thus, for some years the Vatican's bitter enmity helped to emasculate the new Italy in the international diplomatic struggle. At home, the opposition of the Church—which forbade the faithful to recognize the new regime, and particularly prohibited their taking part in national elections—made difficult any justification of the State in the minds of a good many Italians. Among sections of the peasantry—attracted perhaps less by pure faith than by superstition—the Church long remained a powerful authority, a state within the State. In local politics, militant and socially-minded priests sometimes were among those who protested against the ruling economic powers. However, the Papacy was not in principle opposed to the existing social scheme. It merely could not give its blessings to the Government that had robbed it of some of its prerogatives.

After unification, too, the patriotic ardor of intellectual circles changed to disappointment over the actual accomplishments of the *Risorgimento*, and to pessimism about Italy's future. Recognition of Italy's military and political weaknesses and its dependence on other Powers was a matter of shame to many. The parliamentary system seemed to reveal an incapacity for even the most modest social reforms. Progress in reducing pestilence and illiteracy was much too slow. The emigration of great numbers of Italian peasants—unable to find a decent place for themselves at home, and received abroad with condescension or contempt—was depressing to sensitive patriots. Nor was the Italian State—the sixth and least important Great Power—held in high esteem in the foreign chancellories. All this made for a profound dissatisfaction with the political system, not only among the working classes (who after all had most to suffer materially from it), but even more significantly among the intellectuals of the middle class. Theirs was a mood of self-torture, a brooding over the alleged political and economic inferiority of the Italian people. They were obsessed by a vision of an Italy leading all the world—and anything short of this meant failure. Italy's regeneration seemed incomplete; it still was spiritually a backward province of museums and ruins, sadly in need of modernization. Some thought to find the means for modernization in the Socialist movement. Others came to seek it in even more passionate exaltation of the Nation, and were inexorably drawn further by dreams of a resurrected Roman Empire.

In the meantime, machine industry began to emerge in North Italy as a powerful social force. Industrialization meant growing concentration of business proprietorship and the rise of a new proletariat.

Development of the factory system was at first slow. Measured by North European standards, technical and organizational knowledge was backward, and the spirit of industrial enterprise was weak and hesitant. The apparatus of credit, too, was primitive. Private capital was limited, and sought the safer field of investment in land and agricultural enterprise. It was the State that supplied the rising Italian industry with shield and sword, and its aid became increasingly generous as time passed. Most important, aside from the maintenance of a legal system congenial to business traffic, was the erection of a tariff wall and the development of other forms of subsidy. Communal and provincial governments helped by donating land and money to business men. The building of railroads and ships, and the growing military and naval establishments, were visible evidence of direct and indirect flow of capital from the State to industry. Foreign capital and technical skill, German, English, Belgian, French, Swiss, also came to help industrialize Italy.

The early free-trade policies of the new Kingdom gave way, first in 1878, then more definitely in 1887, to industrial protectionism. To be sure, the well-being of the peasants demanded free trade: full opportunity to exchange their wines, olive oil, fruits, and vegetables for the cheaply manufactured goods of Northern and Western Europe. The State, however, was bent on enlarging and reserving home markets for the products of the industrialists of North Italy, and in extending their fields of profitable business abroad. This called for tariffs and the levying of heavy taxes for the development of the nation's armed forces. But industrial tariffs were countered abroad by retaliatory duties levelled against Italian farm exports. The years immediately following 1887 were critical for Italian agriculture, squeezed out of an important foreign market by French tariffs, and exposed to keen competition in the home market from the farmers of the New World. Soon, to be sure, the grain-producing landlords were to be helped by a tariff on wheat.

Industrial enterprise, aided by the State and a cheap labor supply, pushed on. As in other countries, the textile manufacturers led the way. Before long, they were supplying much of the domestic market and were pushing vigorously into foreign fields. Then with the installation of coke-smelting works and steel furnaces, the basis of the iron and steel industry was laid. And by 1900 machine-making, hydro-electric power production, sugar refining, rubber, cement, and chemical manufacturing were well established in North Italy. Imports rose, in large part because of Italy's dependence on foreign coal, cotton, and metals, but her industries were also finding outlets abroad. Big corporations began to emerge, and the names of captains of industry won prominence. But in Italy, poor in essential raw materials, heavy industry from the beginning took on an exceptionally parasitic character. What it lacked in natural advantages it made up in special privileges accorded by Government purchases and tariff protection, and in the cheapness of labor.

Industrialization of course produced important social and political changes. The significance of landed possessions tended to decline. Landlords edged over to make room for the propertied men of industry. The dominance of North Italy over the rest of the country was emphasized still more. Protectionist tariff policies weighed most of all on the Southern peasants. The military, naval, and communications policies of the State—its eyes fixed on the strategic Alpine frontiers—gave preference to the North. The rise of huge industrial and financial stock companies, in which Southern landlords placed their savings, shifted precious capital away from the South.

Moreover, factories created an urban working class. At first the industrial workers were a part of the agricultural population—men and women who left the fields temporarily for jobs in the mills. As time passed, however, there arose a distinct and permanent community of factory hands, not subjected so easily as the rural workers to the old discipline, and indulging in thoughts dangerous to the established order.

Machines were indeed a blessing to their owners. But, at least in the beginning, they were cruel tyrants over the men and women who tended them. The lot of the workers under early Italian industrialism was a miserable one. For long hours of tedious labor in unhealthful mills and shops they were paid incredibly low wages. In the '70s a day's work brought adult mill hands the equivalent of twenty, fifteen, sometimes only twelve cents. And children got as little as six cents. Twelve, fourteen, and even sixteen hours of work each day were common. Child labor was widespread in the textile industries. At the end of the century working conditions were little improved. Starvation wages and exhaustingly long hours were still the rule. The life of the factory workers was as bad as that of the landless peasants laboring in the fields.

But the industrious masses were not blind to their miseries. Gradually they came to strike out in protest against their small share in the national wealth, against their social inferiority and political subjection. Met on every hand by employers and Government with indifference, even with hostility, the workers in towns and villages began to act for themselves. Subversive ideas, Anarchist and Socialist, came from abroad to inspire mass organization and attacks on the going order. Factory workers, also many peasants and field laborers and even minor governmental employees, were swept into an insurgent labor movement. Desperate revolts burst out with growing frequency, and were suppressed only after harsh counter-attacks by the military.

In the '80s and '90s the proletarian movement, increasingly penetrated by Socialist ideas, began to take more stable form in union organizations. Local 'leagues of resistance' and labor councils sprang up in villages and towns to aid striking workmen. The early trade unions led a precarious life outside the law. Employers and their allies felt themselves seriously threatened by this open challenge to the traditional despotism of farm and factory. They called on police and courts for help. The Government, armed with power to dissolve societies 'disturbing the economic peace,' was commanded by men who believed in using this power for the outright crushing of all union activity. Employers resisted the demands of organized labor directly, too, by well-timed lockouts, and for a time in the '90s succeeded in driving down wage rates. They refused to treat with union leaders, insisting on all their old rights. They bitterly opposed demands that the Government change its policy and intervene in the interests of the workers. 'With the intervention of the State into private business affairs,' wrote a textile master, 'we seriously fear that those sentiments of mutual love and respect generally prevailing between employers and workers in this country will be destroyed. Mistrust, frictions, and divisions will arise. And this can easily lead to strikes, today so rare, resulting in serious damage to all.'[1]

At the end of the century, however, the policy of the naked fist—which, in the face of growing popular resistance, meant ever more bloodshed and terror, and possibly even revolution beyond—was abandoned. The Government, obliged to recognize the legality of unions, adopted a more tolerant attitude. Now labor organizations spread rapidly. Local unions were banded together in provincial federations, and soon a nation-wide league of unions was founded. By 1909, some 320,000 workers were associated with this league, the General Confederation of Labor. Socialists were prominent in the Confederation, but it declined to identify itself officially with a political party. It saw its mission to be the extension and support of unions struggling towards the immediate goal of better working conditions. This was to be reinforced by a policy aimed at obtaining parliamentary concessions. From the outset, then, the main body of organized labor, although frequently avowing an ultimate aim of achieving Socialism, was opportunistic and reformist rather than revolutionary. More impatient, violently inclined workers, however, joined a Syndicalist Union, committed to a program of direct action. Revolutionary syndicalism, with its mistrust of parliamentary and international tactics, and its emphasis on class warfare and the general strike, was to play an important part in shaping the Italian labor movement. During the '90s, too, unions were founded by Catholics, inspired by the Christian reformism of Leo XIII's *Rerum novarum*. Their major following came from among the small landholding peasantry, share-tenants, and textile workers (largely part-time rural workers) mindful of the ancient virtues. Their program ran in terms of an extension of petty proprietorship, a strengthening of the co-operative movement, and development of peaceful 'class-collaboration' within the existing social framework.

It was in North and Central Italy that the unions first took root, and these regions remained their main field of action. They had only limited successes in the South. There, the discontent of the poor peasantry found relief in emigration.

A mass movement to the New World began in the '80s, and in the following twenty-five years it became a human avalanche. This reduction of the labor supply at home, and the savings sent or brought back by emigrants, did very much to improve living conditions in the South. Indeed, emigration was of enormous importance not only in building up Italy economically, but also in bringing about a political and cultural transformation of the masses.

Elsewhere in Italy the labor organizations took the offensive against employers in aggressively fought strikes and boycotts. They sought collective agreements assuring higher wages, a shorter working day, control over hiring methods and over the use of labor-displacing techniques and machines. In their struggles, and especially in their readiness to join in sympathetic strikes, the Italian workers gave proof of impassioned devotion and self-sacrifice. More and more, employers were forced to submit to contracts that brought better working conditions. As time passed, however, they began to organize labor-fighting associations.

The unions took the lead in establishing co-operative companies engaged in farming, manufacturing, marketing, banking—that is, in almost every conceivable field. The co-operatives, in turn, rendered valuable services to the working-class movement, backing up strikes, cutting costs of living, spreading union ideas, and helping to recruit members. Also, many unions supported evening schools, lending libraries, reading rooms, amateur musical and dramatic companies, and these did much to raise the cultural level of the workers. The labor councils—the municipal centers of trade unions—came to play an increasingly forceful role in local politics.

The militant labor unions and emigration led to a substantial rise of living standards throughout the country. The purchasing power of the daily wages of farm laborers, for example, advanced about forty per cent during the decade before the World War. Working hours, too, were reduced. Furthermore, labor representatives and sympathizers in the National Parliament did much to develop social-reform legislation. Their pressure led to laws extending the suffrage to all adult males, prohibiting child labor, establishing compulsory industrial-accident insurance and maternity-aid funds, and providing for free distribution of quinine in malarial regions. Finally, the Socialist movement familiarized the workers—and also many members of the upper classes—with the great social and economic problems of the day. It was the Socialists who awakened the common men and gave them organization, more self-confidence, and new hopes.

The ranks of Socialism were recruited from among factory workers, farm laborers, and small peasants. Yet its chiefs were almost exclusively lawyers and professors. That is, its leadership was essentially intellectual and academic, and in important ways remained apart from the workers and peasants. With the entrance of Socialists into the parliamentary system and with their growing legislative effectiveness, the leaders gradually turned away from the earlier revolutionary outlook towards a mild reformism.

Economically and culturally, Italy was making rapid strides during the last fifteen years before the World War. Certainly, in the face of much real progress, the pessimism of the intellectuals was not fully justified. Italian business enterprise was steadily developing in range and intensity. Factory output continued to grow. Large-scale automobile production came into being; the Italian merchant marine rose to fourth place in Europe; foreign trade expanded. Great stock companies became more and more dominant. And the processes of

financial consolidation of business were facilitated by big banking houses.

The rise of industrialism had 'spiritual' repercussions, too.
Systematic business enterprise, using large-scale machine
techniques for its own purposes, put a premium on aggressive
activity, on acquisitive individualism, on the immediately
useful and gainful. Such values must be accepted if 'backward' Italy—traditionally the land of museums, bell towers,
and flower gardens—were to be 'modernized.' Pragmatic
philosophical attitudes and an art of mobility and violence
fell in with this mood. The social significance of the new intellectual currents, pointing toward a 'modern' Italy, lay in
their reinforcing the pressure of industrialism to find wider
market outlets at home and abroad. Only low labor costs,
State subsidies, and monopolized home markets could enable
Italian machine industry to reach a level comparable to that
of the Northern capitalist countries, more advanced technically and supplied with cheaper coal and iron. The growing
power of the industrial and financial classes found further expression politically—in a militant Nationalist Party, in more
aggressive diplomacy, in expansion of armaments.

The active personalities in the new Nationalist movement
—founded in 1910—came at first almost entirely from the intellectual *élite*, but its point of view had wide influence in the
upper middle class. Essentially, it stood for warlike, imperial-
ist policies and for a complete break with the Italy of tradition. From the beginning it was opposed to the parliamentary
regime and to the Socialist labor movement. Only the young
possess the future, and only in war can a nation find its soul—
so ran the Nationalist creed. Italy, *all* Italy, is a proletarian
nation. It is poor, and therefore despised and exploited by
other nations. Italy's equality can be won only in struggle

with the exploiting nations. Italy has a sacred right to conquer bread and land abroad for its own sons. And perhaps all the better if that must mean war.

To the skeptically-minded all this must have been a new mythology, designed to blot out domestic social conflict, to confuse and frighten critics of the existing order by appealing for nation-wide solidarity against foreign enemies.

Turkey's dying empire offered a first test for the rising Italian imperialism. The Tripolitan War, in 1911, was a decisive break with the folk-lore of the *Risorgimento*, that is, with its professed ideals of liberalism and humanitarianism, world peace and brotherhood. A patriotic hysteria gripped many people. A little military glory was tasted, and it was found good. Moreover, it might incidentally be useful in winning outlets for men and merchandise. Even a number of Socialists succumbed, arguing that Italians, too, must carry a white man's burden.

Soon, the outbreak of the World War forced another choice between war and peace. At first, neutrality seemed the only reasonable course to the great majority of politically vocal Italians. Many big business men and financiers were opposed to intervention. And the masses of the population had no desire to take up arms. But war did finally come, in early 1915. For this, all the conscious and unconscious hyper-nationalists among the intellectuals and the civil and military bureaucracy were responsible. They cloaked their lust for war and empire —their 'sacred egoism'—in the old popular mythology of patriotism. The sons of Italy beyond the frontiers must be brought into the national fold. This was the alleged glorious mission of war. Underneath the patriotic slogans, however, was the need for a war that would feed the appetites of the imperialists. In these terms the price offered by the Western

Powers for Italy's arms seemed bigger than that bid by Austria and Germany. 'Sacred egoism' chose the side that made
the most generous promises.

Peasants and workers, despite the protest of Socialists and
Catholics, obeyed the call to battle in the name of democracy
and 'unredeemed Italy.' It was, of course, they who bore the
major burden of a war whose spiritual purposes they could
not comprehend. They sacrificed not only their lives in the
trenches but also their daily bread at home. As the months of
bloody stalemate dragged on, however, protest against the
slaughter mounted. Among the peasant soldiers, a deadly
war-weariness set in. Behind the lines, all the old social ani-
mosities were intensified. The war produced further upheaval
among the peasantry. It stirred them up, gave them new per-
spectives, and thus accelerated changes that emigration had
begun. Conviction grew among the masses that they were
suffering and dying in order to safeguard and even to swell the
riches of landlords, factory owners, bankers. More and more,
they demanded that the fields they cultivated be given to them
and that industry be controlled in their interest. This must
be the compensation for their sacrifices.

The rising wave of popular dissent was held back by the ex-
hortations and promises of politicians. It was expedient for
leaders of the Government, desperately pressed by the enemy
and uncertain of the continued loyalty of its own soldiers, to
say that the demands of peasants and workers would be
granted—at the end of the war. Their promises were big but
vague: the great landed estates would be divided among the
landless rural workers, and profit-sharing and factory control
would be introduced for the benefit of industrial workers. All
this would come, once victory was won.

In the meantime, however, the war was a powerful stimulus

to the further expansion and concentration of industrial enterprise. Foreign and domestic competition was greatly reduced. The State was ready to pay high prices for the machines and munitions it needed so urgently. To this end also it encouraged the large business combinations to expand their financial and technical controls. Huge stock companies—*Fiat, Montecatini, Breda, Ilva, Ansaldo*—became ever more powerful. The capitalization of the machine-making firms tripled between 1914 and 1919. The chemical industry, set up largely for the production of agricultural fertilizers, now turned to the manufacture of explosives, drugs, synthetic dyes, and oils. Reduced access to British coal stimulated the output of hydro-electric power. Investments in the power industry and consumption of electricity doubled. Formal and informal agreements between State and business organs became increasingly important in the structure of the industrial system. Monopolistic devices, developed through communities of interest, trade associations, syndicates, and cartels, and through governmental agencies, largely displaced competitive tactics in the control of markets. Agricultural enterprise, too, bore the imprint of industrialization. In the North, especially, more emphasis was put on the use of machinery and on commercial crops.

The war thus hastened the pace of Italian industrialism. Business enterprise and the State penetrated each other to a degree unknown before. And, needless to say, the war was a period of big profits for industrialists and financiers.

The defeat of Austria brought a brief moment of patriotic exaltation. But the celebration of victory soon gave way to bitter disappointment over the fruits of the terrible combat. Disillusionment was shared by people of all classes. The prophets of imperialism saw angrily that the peace treaties would give Italy far less than they had been led to expect. *Rentiers* and salaried employees, whose wealth and incomes had shrunk during the years of war, now found that the hidden taxes of inflation were impoverishing them still further. And workers learned that the promises of land and industrial democracy were hollow. For these disappointments the existing political system was blamed. In all classes, too, there were men—conditioned by the war to violence—ready to throw over parliamentary processes and to use force in order to win their ends.

Within a year after the Armistice occurred two events that were to be decisive in shaping the future of Italy. One revealed the helplessness of the Government to meet an armed challenge from the Right. The other brought revolution from the Left visibly nearer.

In September 1919, Fiume, an Adriatic seaport city formerly belonging to Hungary, was seized in defiance of the peace-makers in Paris and of the Government in Rome by a motley band of Italian adventurers and idealists. They were led by a famous poet of exotic tastes and, more significant, they were aided by active army officers. Fiume, its political status still undecided by the victorious Powers, was claimed for Italy by the Nationalists because of its predominantly Italian population. For many months the Government could not oust the usurpers. Its commands went unheeded, and it was unable to count on the loyalty of its own generals. This apparent impotence suggested to many that similar adventures nearer home would not be resisted, and might even be reinforced, by the military.

In November 1919, a general election took place. The Socialists, campaigning with definitely revolutionary appeals, captured a third of all the votes cast. Furthermore, a remarkably large following was won by the recently founded Catholic

Populist Party, also avowing radical purposes. The machinery of parliamentary democracy clearly was being used by the proletarians for their own ends. To the established order this meant that social overturn could not long be held off—unless counter-attack were quickly launched. The Socialists joyfully announced: 'Revolutionary Italy is born!'

## II : THE BLACKSHIRT REVOLUTION

AFTER a long and bitter struggle, Italy had won her war with Austria. Yet the Armistice did not bring social peace. Instead, the old struggle for political and economic power, intensified by the strain of war, plunged the country into a deep crisis.

The end of the war found Italy impoverished in morale, materials, and manpower. The people felt themselves to be, not conquerors, but conquered. Home-coming soldiers were treated with scant respect by many who had consistently opposed the war. Thousands of officers were suddenly turned loose, and found it hard to resign themselves to the fact that they were no longer in positions of authority. The politicians of the old school tried to take up their game where they had left it in 1915. But the traditional political methods were not to the liking of men who had learned new ways and new outlooks at the front.

Much of the apparatus of industrial and agricultural production had been directed to the needs of the army. Only with difficulty could it be readjusted to a peace-time tempo. The battle-scarred regions in the North had to be repaired. Elsewhere, important productive equipment—such as that of the farms and railways—was much in need of renovation. Vested interest groups among the industrialists, bankers, organized workers, and co-operatives, had profited during the war from State controls and subsidies. They continued to demand financial aid from the Government. Thus the war-time subventions carried on. As a result of these and other burdens inherited from the conflict, the State's expenditures ran far ahead of revenues. Inflationary borrowing was necessary. The monetary system was also weakened by a concurrent rise of merchandise imports and shrinkage of income from emigrant remittances and tourist expenditures. Heavy taxes and rising prices meant further hardships for the middle and lower classes. But inflation also induced a speculative fever. The rise of values led to unsound lending, and in the collapse that followed a number of important banks failed. Industrial output sank to a level lower than that of 1913.

Nothing came of the politicians' promise to divide the big landed estates among the peasants. But a considerable amount of land was acquired by urban speculators and war-profiteers, and also by small farmers who had gained wealth during the war. Thus, newly enriched elements of the middle class came to reinforce the older propertied groups.

These post-war troubles gave a fresh impetus to the movements of dissent. The disillusionment caused by the peace treaties, the revelation of big profits made by the war-suppliers, the muddling impotence of governmental processes, the success of the Russian Revolution—all strengthened a widespread belief that return to pre-war conditions was impossible, that sweeping social reforms were necessary. A more immediate spur to popular discontent was the soaring cost of living.

The great gains of the left-wing parties in the election of 1919 reflected the temper of the masses of the people. Not for nothing had they hungered, bled, and died in the hard years of the war. Now they seemed to roar: We will remake Italy into our own democracy!

The numerical strength of the unions rose tremendously. The General Confederation of Labor, which had comprised about 300,000 workers in 1914, advanced to 1,375,000 in 1919, and to 2,300,000 in 1920. The membership of the Catholic unions increased to nearly two millions, while syndicalist and other lesser unions were said to have 700,000 members. And this growth was quite as impressive in the countryside as in the cities. For example, a quarter of the followers of the General Confederation in 1920 were peasants and rural workers.

The Socialist Party's enrolled membership rose to 200,000, as against 50,000 before the war. Its candidates in the 1919 election received 1,840,000 votes, compared with 3,500,000 for those of all other parties. The number of Socialist deputies in the National Parliament was tripled. The Party's strength was of course most pronounced in the industrial North, where it won forty to sixty per cent of the electors. Many town and district governments were captured by the Socialists. In 1920, a quarter of all the communes and provinces in the country were under their control.

The official phrases of the Party became bolder. Moscow's rhetoric was echoed in Italy. Italian Socialists took part in the founding of the Communist International in 1920, and announced their intention to swing Italy over to the principles of the Bolshevist Revolution. A Party congress in Bologna announced: 'Inasmuch as no ruling class has ever renounced its own despotic powers except under the compulsion of violence, we are convinced that the proletariat must use violence in order to win power. Only the dictatorship of the proletariat can bring about the disappearance of classes and of capitalism.' [1] This was quite enough to send shudders through all traditionally-minded men. Significantly, however, the demands of the unions were more modest. The program of the General Confederation called for workers' participation in the control of industry, the eight-hour day, an extension of social insurance, heavy progressive income taxes and a confiscation of excess war-profits, gradual nationalization of the land, and cultivation of farms and execution of public works by labor co-operatives. Despite their occasionally violent language, most of the Socialists were firm believers in orderly, democratic government and were resolved to advance within the framework of the law.

Beside the Socialists another party basing itself on mass appeals now pushed forward—the Catholic Populists. The Papal ban on participation by Catholics in national politics was withdrawn shortly before the war. Early in 1919 a number of priests and Catholic laymen organized the new party. It was astonishingly successful at the polls in November, winning a large following of peasant proprietors, share-tenants, and conservatively inclined wage-workers. Ninety-nine Populist deputies were elected. Its inspirers, disturbed by the menacing specter of Socialism, sought to capture votes from the proletarian and lower middle-class groups by proposing mild reforms that would leave the foundations of the existing temporal and spiritual structure unaltered. Local political autonomy, an extension of petty proprietorship and co-operation, friendly 'class-collaboration' between employers and workers, a peaceful foreign policy in the spirit of the League of Nations —these were the avowed goals. Many of the Populist leaders were genuinely concerned with the popular well-being, and a few, indeed, outdid the Socialists in their zeal for reform. But in the main the party was essentially conservative. Its practical effect was to split the forces of discontent and so to reinforce the existing social system.

The victories of the radical and pseudo-radical parties were promptly reflected in parliamentary action. New laws recognized the principle of collective contracts, extended social-insurance benefits to the unemployed, disabled, and aged, and provided for public aid to the workers' co-operatives. Projects were also drawn up for the establishment of a health-insurance scheme, and for the division of great landed estates among the peasants.

But the working-class movement was not confined to the election of radical orators to office. The insurgent spirit of the times manifested itself more directly in a frontal attack on business and landed property rights, in a wave of agricultural and industrial strikes, and in the seizure of landlords' estates by peasants. The unions used their mass pressure to force employers to grant better working conditions. Cities and villages were rocked by strikes on an unprecedented scale. The number of man-days spent in strikes averaged 4 millions during 1911–14; it rose to 22 millions in 1919, and to more than 30 millions in 1920. (Yet the post-war strikes in Italy were no more widespread than those in England, France, and the United States.)

These aggressive attacks pushed up wage rates, shortened the working day, and forced employers to submit to further union controls over the hiring and dismissal of workers. But it was not only factory and farm wage-workers who won advantages. Unionized share-tenants, too, forced landlords to grant contracts giving them greater independence in management, more secure tenure, and larger shares of the crops. Under pressure of the left-wing parties the Government took steps to curb rising land-rents and to prevent landlords from ousting tenants. Employees' committees obtained the right to supervise the application of collective contracts. Not content with this, the unions demanded that these committees be given at least partial control over industrial policies. The working-class co-operatives were strengthened. They received encouragement from the Government, which supplied them with cheap credit and public lands at low rentals.

In the North the strikes were accompanied by attacks on traders and others who were blamed for high living costs. This included not only intervention in the fixing of retail prices by local, radical-dominated governments, but also, to a limited extent, the plundering of shops by mobs. In Sicily, Calabria, and in the neighborhood of Rome, members of peasant unions and co-operatives invaded many large *latifondi* and put the land under cultivation for their own purposes.

The ruling groups and their governmental representatives were at first hesitant before the threatening masses. Employers felt themselves obliged to grant the demands of the unions. The pillaging of shops and the land-seizures of course alarmed the conservatives greatly, but little or no resistance was offered. Indeed, the Government gave the peasants' actions a measure of legal recognition by setting up a machinery for orderly transfer of uncultivated land to rural co-operatives. At the same time, it tried to prevent further seizures. Although little of tangible importance was actually granted in this way, many peasants believed that the first step towards division of the land had at last been taken.

Thus, in the middle of 1920 the country seemed to be in the first stage of a violent social upheaval. In reality, there was little likelihood of revolution. But industrial and landed proprietorship affected to see its interests menaced to the core.

Fortunately for the conservatives, the left-wing parties and the labor unions were not nearly so strong nor so revolutionary as they appeared. The Catholic Populists talked of reform, but they wanted reform to come peacefully and without fundamental change in the social structure. They were an important anti-revolutionary bloc from the beginning. As for the Socialist Party, the numerical strength of its following gave it a formidable appearance. But it had little internal strength. Its leaders were split by wide differences of opinion as to the method of socializing Italy. Some favored direct and violent mass revolution, perhaps without knowing precisely what they wanted. But the majority counselled piecemeal reforms and a biding of decisive action until the day when capitalism must collapse under its own dead weight. At that moment, the well-ordered Socialist municipal governments, co-operatives, and labor councils would take command. Many Socialists, indeed, were no less opposed to a rapid social overturn than were the Populists. Their argument was a rational one. But they did not realize what changes the war had made in the temper of the people. They aggravated many of the recently discharged soldiers, and at the very time when the attitude of the veterans was of crucial importance. The old-line Socialists overemphasized the function of pedagogues, and ignored the importance of missionaries.

Among the rank-and-file followers of the Socialist Party, however, there was little of the patience needed for a program of attrition. Emotional symbols, not cool argument, were decisive. Many people had been won over to the movement by a belief that Socialism would bring about an immediate righting of the wrongs under which they suffered. This, rather than a conviction that justice must come surely and slowly, held them to the Party. They could as easily be converted into enthusiastic followers of politicians speaking another, and bolder, language.

The fundamental weakness of Italian Socialism was exposed in September 1920. A dispute over wage rates broke out between employers and union workers in the machinery industry of North Italy. The employers threatened a lockout, and the union officials replied to this by ordering the workers to occupy the plants. In consequence, half a million men stayed in some six hundred factories, ousted the employers and their agents, raised red flags, and attempted to continue operations independently. The occupation took place quietly. There was little violence, the workers maintained discipline, and the police and military did not intervene. To many it appeared that the long-heralded proletarian revolution had begun. At last had come the day when the workers would take the means of production into their own hands! The whole country waited tensely for the next move of the strikers, of the millions of other organized workers, and of their leaders.

Had the Socialist chiefs been ready to seize political power at this moment, they might well have been successful. No one seemed to stand in their way. But the leadership of the Party was not prepared for such a decision. On the contrary, it was divided and uncertain. The occupation had begun as merely one further bargaining move in the effort to improve working conditions within the going system. The very opportunity for which the Socialists claimed to have been struggling so long, the opportunity of capturing the State for the workers, had come all too soon. No—it was argued—Italy was not yet ready for a new social order.

In the meantime, while the Socialist and union officials hesitated and disputed, and while the Government remained passive, the 'stay-in' strikers were hard put to operate the factories. Unable to get the necessary working capital and technical assistance, they faced a virtual counter-strike on the part of propertied interests. Finally, the occupation collapsed. The workers went back to their old jobs, disappointed with their leadership. A compromise solution proposed by the

Government was accepted by the trade-union officials and the industrialists. It called for evacuation of the plants, in return for a promise by the owners to allow their employees to share in the control of the enterprises. But the promise was an empty one, and the 'compromise' proved to be little more than a face-saving device to cover up the defeat of the unions.

Everywhere it was sensed that the radical movement had failed, and that it had failed because the leading party of social reform lacked the will to win. The confidence of the masses in Socialism began to ebb.

Now the counter-attack of partisans of the old order began in earnest. From their standpoint, the compromising, delaying tactics of parliamentarianism had once again saved the day. Certainly, the failure of the stay-in strike had given pause to the radical movement. But the end of the traditional regime had come too perilously close. Socialism and the unions were still powerful, and perhaps were now merely gathering new strength and new leadership to strike another, and mightier blow. Clearly, the salvation of men of property lay in a complete and final shattering of the whole movement of social reform. This could be done only outside the parliamentary system, for the votes of Socialists and their sympathizers were much too numerous. It could be done only by sweeping aside all pretense at popular government—that is—by changing the political façade of the State. Nor need this be difficult in terms of armed force. D'Annunzio's occupation of Fiume had shown how little the avowedly liberal parliamentary regime could rely on the military for its defense. At the same time, however, some show of popular approval for such anti-popular actions must be won. This might be achieved by a frenzied beating of the drums of nationalism, accompanied by a few false notes on the trumpets of revolution. Force and terror, in the name of the higher spiritual goals of the nation, were to be the means of destroying the left-wing movement. Such a logic was hardly preconceived. Rather, in the beginning the Socialists and their followers were merely held to be in need of a severe 'lesson.' The rest came as a necessary but unpredicted consequence of the unleashing of violent forces.

The weapon of counter-attack was already at hand. A loose-knit but aggressive body of adventurers, calling themselves *fascisti*, were ready to do the job of breaking Socialist power.

At Milan early in 1915, a little company of revolutionary syndicalists, nationalistic intellectuals, and Futurists—all of them favoring Italian intervention in the war—had organized a 'group for revolutionary action,' the *Fascio di Azione rivoluzionaria*. They were but one of a number of similar interventionist *fasci* springing up elsewhere in the country. Their program was simple enough; they were against Austria, the bourgeoisie, the priests, and Socialism.

Four months after the Armistice the restless, ambitious men of the Milan *fascio* met again to formulate another program suited to the times. Their ranks were now swelled by demobilized soldiers yearning for the life of the battlefront, by old revolutionaries disowned by the Socialists but still looking for masses to lead, by impetuous boys with a longing for violent adventure. In other parts of the country—but especially in the North—men of similar character were also organizing hyper-patriotic *fasci di combattimento*. The main sport of these 'fighting groups' was chauvinistic flag-waving and denunciation of the left-wing political and labor bodies. Common to all the *fascisti* was a hunger for glory and power, and a will to win whatever the means.

And the leader of the Milanese *fascio*, soon to be known as the chief of all the Fascists, was a man with an overwhelming lust for power.

Benito Mussolini, like other Italians of his age, had come out of the village masses in the years before the war to preach and act in the rising struggle against poverty and tyranny. Like others, he had learned—perhaps without ever thinking deeply—the clichés of revolutionary Socialism. He stood out from among his colleagues in his unusual flair for boldly whipping up the emotions of the crowd, whether by the melodramatic gestures of the orator, or by the flaming pen of the sensational journalist. One thing he realized better than others was what he himself wanted of life. To Mussolini life meant above all else opportunity for self-realization in power. And this idea was strengthened by all that he learned—at first- or second-hand—from the works of Machiavelli, Nietzsche, Pareto, Georges Sorel, the Nationalists and Futurists. He knew but one course of action: to seek and win *power* by any road that might lead to it.

At a time when the left-wing movement seemed to offer scope for action and a future to such a man, Mussolini played the part of the violent proletarian revolutionary. Thus, during the Tripolitan war he was internationalist and rabidly antimilitarist. He organized strikes of protest against the war, declared that by fighting in the interests of the workers he was a true patriot, and was imprisoned for several months. The youthful Mussolini was an impassioned foe of all the pillars of the traditional social order. He frantically denounced almost everything that his own Fascism came to represent: militarism and war, colonial adventure, suppression of economic and political democracy, the absolutism of the State. He found it possible to exclaim: 'Down with the State in all its forms and incarnations! . . . The national flag is a rag to be

planted on a dung-hill! . . . Militarism! here is the mon-
strous polyp with a thousand viscous tentacles that sucks increasingly the blood and best energies of peoples! . . . Italy
needed bread and she was bled white by an army and a navy.
She needed to regenerate herself completely and she was
plunged into colonial enterprises. . . . Imagine an Italy in
which thirty-six million citizens should all think in the same
way, as though their brains were cast in the same mold and
you would have . . . a kingdom of boredom and imbecility.'[2]
Young Mussolini's anti-religious tirades made him the target
of clerical newspapers, by which he was labelled 'thug,'
'clown,' and 'desperado.' Wherever he moved he was known
to the police as a dangerous character. Once he complained of
the inquisitive police: 'Is not this persecution of ideas sincerely
professed revolting?'[3] He glorified political assassinations, de-
sertion from the army, the general strike—any and every form
of direct action against employers and the State. And he was
not above practicing some of the ideas that he preached, as
witness his arrests, deportations, and jail sentences. Indeed,
his views on patriotism, religion, parliamentary government, the use of violence, the tactics of revolution, were far
more extreme than those of most of his Socialist contempo-
raries. His advocacy of terror sometimes even appalled them.
But his zeal and energy, his indifference to material rewards,
his talents in journalism and politics, impressed his colleagues
and even endeared him to some. His well-informed, if not
very original, mind awed the humble men for whom he
seemed to be fighting. Never, apparently, was he suspected of
being a mere 'careerist.'

Mussolini the Socialist, however, was fundamentally the
same as Mussolini the Fascist. He always scorned the ideals
and tactics of democracy, liberalism, humanitarianism. Al-

ways he was an apologist of terror, so long as it could help to win his goal. By such a man the forces of violence could as easily be used to crush as to promote the movement of the masses. For the core of Mussolini is an overwhelming urge to assert his ego. 'Yes,' he once admitted, 'I am possessed by this mania. It inflames, gnaws, and consumes me like a physical malady. I want to make a mark on history with my will, like a lion with his claws.' [4]

When the World War came Mussolini was editor of the *Avanti!*, the leading Socialist newspaper in Italy. At first he insisted that Italy must stand aloof from this war of imperialistic powers. Then suddenly, after the battle of the Marne, Mussolini swung completely over into the camp of the interventionists. Now he argued that the ultimate well-being of the Italian masses demanded that Italy fight Austria, for war must hasten social revolution. This about-face led to his expulsion from the Socialist Party. It is frequently said that French money enabled him to set up his own newspaper, the *Popolo d'Italia*, as a vehicle for interventionist propaganda. But it is hardly likely that this could have been sufficient reason for his decision to repudiate his Socialist allegiance. He must have sensed that Italy would in any case enter the conflict, and that in the new situation created by war, his future must be brighter outside the ranks of internationalist, pacifist Socialism. In defending himself against the charge that he had betrayed his old comrades, he prophetically warned them, 'In a few years the Italian masses will follow and applaud me, when you will no longer speak nor have a following.' [5]

Indeed, Mussolini continued during the war and afterwards to pose as a champion of the underprivileged workers. He and his Fascists attempted to rival the Socialists and Populists in

demagogic appeals for social reform. Mussolini wrote in 1919:
'We are taking action not against the working class, but for
it.' [6] He applauded workers' violence against extortionate
tradesmen, even supported occupation of the factories and the
land seizures. His newspaper advised the mob: 'A few profiteers hanged on lamp-posts, a few receivers of stolen goods
squashed under the potatoes or lard that they want to hide,
will serve as an example.' [7] The striking workmen of Dal-
mine, who in March 1919 occupied their employer's plant
and continued to operate it, won his praise: 'You have taken
a class position, but you have not forgotten the nation. You
might have struck in a negative and destructive manner. But
thinking of the interests of the people you have begun a
creative strike, one that does not interrupt production.' [8]
Shortly thereafter he thundered: 'We demand expropriation
of the land, the mines and the transportation system. We support completely and absolutely the just demands of the peasants, miners, railroad workers and sailors.' [9] And during the
occupation of the factories in 1920 he wrote in his newspaper:
'What has arrived in Italy is a revolution, or better said, a
phase of the revolution that we began in 1915. There are no
street battles or barricades. But a legal relationship, several
centuries old, has been broken. The worker has conquered the
right to control the economic activity in which he takes part.' [10]
    The program adopted by the Fascists in 1919 was a mix-
ture of catchwords borrowed from Republicans, Nationalists,
and Socialists. It called for universal suffrage for both men
and women, election of a national assembly that should prepare a new constitution, abolition of the Senate, establishment
of a national militia. In economic matters the program was
more extreme, demanding the nationalization of arms and
munitions factories, control of other factories, railroads, and

public services by workers' councils, minimum wages and the universal eight-hour day, extension of social insurance, confiscation of war-profits and of certain Church properties, heavy inheritance and income taxes. 'We have so little concern for the bourgeoisie,' said Mussolini, 'that we have put at the head of our program a demand for expropriation of large private fortunes, for confiscation of war-time super-profits, for heavy taxation of capital. We will accept no form of dictatorship.' [11] Yet commitment to a formal program never weighed heavily on his conscience. In 1922 he declared that 'Fascism is not a museum of dogmas and principles.' Indeed, this was probably a real advantage, for it permitted an easy shifting with the political winds and finally enabled the Fascists to recruit followers among all social classes.

Despite these efforts to win converts among the working people, the Fascists at first had little success in attracting a widespread following. In the campaign preceding the election of November 1919 they competed with the Socialists and Populists in demands for economic and political reconstruction. But the election disappointed them, for they did not win a single seat in Parliament. In Milan, Mussolini received only 5,000 of the 268,000 votes cast. *Fascismo*, it appeared, was drowned in the flood-tide of Socialism. No wonder that Mussolini exclaimed early in 1920: 'Down with the Bourgeois State! down with the Socialist State! From now on we—the last survivors of individualism—shall have only the absurd but always consoling faith of anarchism!' [12]

The election did, however, reveal the greatly increased political strength of the left-wing forces. The men of business and landed property and their followers were seriously perturbed. And the strikes, the gains in working conditions won by the unions, and the new social legislation turned anxiety

into panic. Sensing the value of hyper-patriotic appeals reinforced by terrorism, they—and especially the magnates of
heavy industry and landed property—turned more and more
to the support of the Fascists. Mussolini continued to talk of
himself as a revolutionary, and to exhort the masses. But at
the same time, he accepted money from industrialists and
agrarians, and told them: 'Do not forget that one of the essential postulates of Fascism is the suppression of all the apparatus of war, of all state intervention in economic affairs, and a
re-establishment of economic liberty, so necessary to the return of normal conditions.' [13] This was also a 'postulate' of the
business men.

Respectable people could tolerate, even patronize, a Fascism that preached *laissez-faire*. The *Corriere della Sera*—
Italy's leading 'liberal' newspaper—confessed: 'We are happy
that one party—whose name everyone knows—has returned
to the old liberal traditions.' [14]

With the collapse of the revolutionary menace, after the unsuccessful seizure of the factories in 1920, the Fascists became
effective (if not wholly deliberate) guards of the propertied
interests. The forces of industrial and landed employers were
organized in two powerful associations. The General Confederation of Industry represented all big industrialists and
most of the smaller ones, and the General Confederation of
Agriculture marshalled 700,000 landowners, including nearly
all the great proprietors. Their maxim was: Maintenance of
private property rights; all power to the employers. The attitude of landed proprietors was expressed in a speech at the
first national convention of landowners, in Bologna in February 1921: 'We are ready to defend our rights . . . not only
to save ourselves, but also in order to defend civilization and
progress. . . . We do not wish to strangle anyone, neither do

we wish to be strangled, for we know that we are defending sacred personal rights and class rights.' [15] Still fearing the labor organizations, the big employers called on the *fascisti* to defend their sacred rights by crushing the menacing unions.

Furthermore, enriched peasants and farmers, small merchants and artisans—that is, men of the rural and urban middle classes who feared the Socialist threat—streamed into the ranks of Fascism. Among the most ardent recruits were peasants who had climbed into the ranks of medium landowners, farm-tenants hating the monopolistic practices of the unions, lawyers and tradesmen who had speculated in land during the inflation period, shop-keepers and craftsmen whose business had been reduced by the Socialist co-operatives, *rentiers* whose incomes were shrinking while the wageworkers' pay was advancing. All became as zealous defenders of the patriotic virtues and of the privileges of property as were the great industrialists and landlords. Moreover, peacefully inclined employers were coerced by their more powerful and more aggressive fellows to contribute against their will to the Fascist cause. Nor must it be forgotten that ardent Blackshirts were recruited among the underprivileged and unemployed workers.

Many of the Fascist sympathizers no doubt were moved by a genuine abhorrence of social disorder and a desire to renovate the political system. They saw in Socialism and the unions a serious menace to domestic peace. Others, disgusted by the apparent impotence of the Government and disappointed at the meager spoils that fell to Italy at the end of the war, were attracted by the nationalistic appeals of Fascism. For them, Fascism would make the dream of a powerful, united Italy come true.

The Blackshirt movement gave the middle classes an ideology, an illusion that they could play an independent part in the control of the country. It exploited the mystical longings of little men for a Saviour. Fascism in its doctrinal catholicity included a strain of reversionary anti-capitalist sentiments, congenial to the hard-pressed lower middle classes. It was grounded on fear of the growing power of corporate industry and finance, and looked toward a restoration of a world of petty tradesmen. More significant, however, was a virulent and selfish hatred of proletarian Socialism, a determination to punish the workers and reduce them to their old and 'proper' status of docile servants.

But at the same time the Fascists organized their own unions, or 'economic syndicates.' These 'mixed' associations of workers, peasants, small traders, and landowners, were an important auxiliary to the movement. They were based on the work of Edmondo Rossoni, who before the war had been like Mussolini a revolutionary Socialist. For a time he was an organizer for the Industrial Workers of the World, in the United States. Returning to Italy when hostilities began, he also became patriotic and in 1918 founded a nationalistic labor union. Its members were largely recruited among rural workers in North and Central Italy. In 1921 Rossoni allied himself with Mussolini, and soon succeeded in building up an apparently formidable Fascist labor organization. By the summer of 1922 it claimed (no doubt with considerable exaggeration) some 800,000 members. Many of its active personalities were old syndicalist revolutionaries. Their presence in the Fascist ranks was due in part to their careerist ambitions, in part to their antipathy towards liberalism, parliamentarism, and democratic Socialism—an emotion that they shared with the Nationalists. They helped serve the Fascist cause by infecting a part of the proletariat with a mistrust of parliamentary methods, with a taste for forceful direct action, with national as opposed to international sentiments. Fascist phrasemakers captured followers among the lower classes with promises of safeguards against competition and exploitation, of security and spiritual elevation into the happy status of 'collaborators in national production.' 'The workers have nothing to fear from Fascism,' it was said. 'Their just rights will be loyally safeguarded.' [16]

Thus Fascism became a mass movement. Its membership grew rapidly, rising during 1920 from 17,000 to about 100,000, reaching 320,000 in the autumn of 1921 (at which time the loosely federated *fasci* were formally organized into a political party), and 477,000 in the summer of 1922.

The rising force of Fascism was based on the money of propertied folk and the manpower and fervor of middle-class and proletarian elements. More important, however: it throve on the toleration and active aid of bureaucrats, army officers, judges, and policemen. Government officials helped prepare the ground for the Blackshirt punitive squads, furnished them with arms, and gave them freedom of action. The official historian of Fascism, Volpe, put it mildly when he wrote: 'Fascism did not lack a certain indulgence from above.' [17] Without help from the civil and military bureaucracy Fascism could not have won power.

Throughout 1921 and 1922 the Fascists waged war against the old labor organizations.

In the agricultural regions of North and Central Italy * the military *fasci*, well armed and equipped, fought directly in the service of the big landowners. They began their offensive with the smashing of 'bolshevistic' peasant and farm labor unions,

---

* Fascism made little impression in the South before the March on Rome.

then turned to the extermination of Catholic and Republican rural associations. Socialists were ousted from local governmental posts, members of the unions were persecuted, workers' meeting-places and co-operatives were destroyed. In the towns, Fascism's attack on organized labor was much the same as in the country. The Blackshirt squadrists proceeded systematically to crush the whole system of unions, whether Socialist or Catholic. They sacked not only union headquarters, but also co-operative stores, workers' libraries and social rooms, radical and liberal newspaper offices and presses. They also undertook to act as strike-breakers. By arresting many anti-Fascists and only a few Fascist terrorists, the police co-operated magnificently. The membership of both Socialist and Catholic unions fell rapidly. Most of the formerly flourishing Socialist co-operatives disappeared. The effectiveness of the Fascist counter-attack was also reflected in the declining number of strikes during 1921–3, and in their less and less favorable outcome for the workers.

The Fascist technique consisted of shouting: 'We are saving our beloved Italy from anarchy and Bolshevism, from immorality and brutal violence.' But Fascism was not fighting Bolshevism. It was fighting liberalism and democracy. It was carrying on the old battle of privileged groups against the masses of their countrymen.

The workers resisted, but their leadership was divided and indecisive. In consequence, their defensive strikes were desultory, weak, and fruitless. Individual workers occasionally fought terror with counter-terror. Certainly they had sufficient provocation, but this merely enabled the better-armed Fascists to strike back with even greater force. The Socialist leaders, however, were unwilling to use any but legal weapons. They counselled the workers: 'Remain in your homes; do not retaliate. Even silence, even cowardice are sometimes heroic.' [18] The defeatism of the Socialists was expressed in their opinion that 'Fascism cannot be conquered by armed, direct action, but only by legal means.' [19] Repeatedly the union officials asked the Government for protection against the Blackshirt onslaughts. Promises were made, but the authorities continually helped the Fascists, either by giving them legal and military assistance or by remaining benevolently neutral. Strikes, speeches, and memoranda of protest were poor weapons with which to repulse the enemy's guns.

Moreover, the Socialist Party was split by internal dissension. The Communist wing broke away in January 1921 to form a new party. To be sure, the Socialists and Communists polled a surprisingly large vote in the national election of 1921, winning 138 seats in the Chamber of Deputies. The Fascists elected only 35 deputies. Mussolini, apparently impressed by the continued popular strength of the left-wing, made efforts to patch up a truce with the Socialists. (Indeed, as late as the autumn of 1922 he was still ready to play with the idea of parliamentary coalition with the Socialists.) But he was no longer able to shift his following to suit his own political tactics. The reactionary Fascist and Nationalist chieftains, and especially those allied with the agrarian gentry, showed that they were quite ready to carry on without Mussolini. Always quick to subordinate principles to the main chance, he yielded. And the terror went on. The early program of the Fascists, with its revolutionary phrases, was toned down as the alliance with big propertied interests was welded. Mussolini also decided that, in view of the necessity of winning the support of the royalist army officers, a monarchy would suit him quite as well as a republic.

Resistance to the Fascists was weakened by continued conflicts within the Socialist ranks, and by the inability of the democratic parties to effect a parliamentary union. In the meantime, the Fascists were penetrating the military and administrative organs of the Government—building a state within the State. The leaders of the national cabinet still held to a policy of petty political manoeuvring and of tolerance towards Fascism. Seemingly they were convinced that the Blackshirts were a useful check on the extremists of the Left, and that if only they could win some political strength they must become moderate and ready to fit themselves into the old parliamentary system. Furthermore, by 1922 the economic situation was much improved. The Government was making good progress towards balancing its income and expenditures, and industrial production and trade were recovering. There were social disorders, it is true, but for this the Fascist terrorists were largely responsible. Certainly the strikes and factory-occupations had not prevented a business revival. Mussolini himself declared that the 'bolshevist peril' no longer existed. It was widely believed that economic recovery would strengthen the more moderate political forces.

But this view was mistaken. Reactionary industrialists and landlords felt no love for the ministers who were rapidly succeeding one another in office, and whom they held responsible for heavy taxes on property and for legislative concessions made to the unions and co-operatives. The men who had supported the Blackshirt terror did not propose merely to re-establish a social equilibrium. Why should they not make the most of an opportunity to destroy Socialism and political liberalism? And the Fascist leaders wanted power for themselves. 'Our program is simple,' Mussolini declared. 'We want to rule Italy.' [20] The Fascists took over control of numerous local governments in the North, and talked openly of an armed seizure of the national Government.

The climax came at the end of October 1922. The police and military allowed the Fascists to occupy police headquarters, railway stations, telegraph offices, and other public buildings in Northern cities. Armed bands of Blackshirts, estimated by various observers at anything from 50,000 to 300,000, began to converge on Rome. On the morning of 28 October when a few thousand of the marchers had nearly reached the city, the cabinet decided to ask the King to decree a state of martial law. Resistance by even a small force of trained soldiers might quickly have dispelled the Blackshirts. 'After five minutes of gunfire,' said General Badoglio, 'Fascism will completely collapse.' [21] But the King refused to sign the proclamation, on the ground that it would precipitate civil war. He knew that certain high army officers were supporting the Fascists and was informed, perhaps incorrectly, that the army could no longer be trusted to fight against them. Also he heard rumors that the Fascists were prepared to place his cousin, the Duke of Aosta, on the throne. Finally, was he really averse to a Fascist victory?

On 29 October Mussolini, who had been waiting in Milan, was called to form a ministry. He rode into Rome, not on horseback, but in a *wagon-lit*. The first act of the Blackshirt revolution was ended.

The General Confederation of Industry, the organ of big business, announced triumphantly three days after the March on Rome: 'The new regime is formed. We look to it with great hopes. We will support the program of this regime with all our strength, for in it, for the first time after long years, a protection of property rights, the general obligation to work, a full valuation of the energy of the individual and of national sentiment are proclaimed energetically.' [22] Hyper-national sentiment was not merely useful to seekers after political office. Its dominance over all alternatives was desperately necessary for the salvation of the ancient vested interests. So thought many respectable men. But this regime to which they looked with great hopes would be no simple servant. It was to go on and on, until it conquered all Italy and stood forth as the pattern of a new social order.

# III : BUILDING THE POLICE STATE

ARISTOTLE in his *Politics* outlined 'the ancient prescriptions for the preservation of a tyranny:'

'The tyrant should lop off all those who are too high; he must put to death men of spirit; he must not allow common meals, clubs, education, and the like; he must be upon his guard against anything which is likely to inspire either courage or confidence among his subjects; he must prohibit literary assemblies or other meetings for discussion, and he must take every means to prevent people from knowing one another (for acquaintance begets mutual confidence). Further, he must compel the inhabitants to appear in public and live at his gates; then he will know what they are doing; if they are always kept under, they will learn to be humble. . . . A tyrant should also endeavour to know what each of his subjects says or does, and should employ spies . . .; for the fear of informers prevents people from speaking their minds, and if they do, they are more easily found out. . . . Also, he should impoverish his subjects; he thus provides money for the support of his guards, and the people, having to keep hard at work, are prevented from conspiring. . . . Another practice of tyrants is to multiply taxes. . . . The tyrant is also fond of making war in order that his subjects may have something to do and be always in want of a leader. . . . Under these three heads the whole policy of a tyrant may be summed up, and to one or another of them all his ideas may be referred: (1) he sows distrust among his subjects; (2) he takes away their power; (3) he humbles them.' [1]

49

These too are the methods of the Fascist Dictatorship. But modern technology—the useful arts of mass persuasion even more than the arts of war—has given tyranny a new endurance.

Stripped of its 'spiritual' avowals, the original, visible purpose of Fascism was to make Italy safe for the traditional ruling groups. To fulfill this mission, the Fascist regime had to shatter the challenging labor movement and those governmental and cultural institutions that might be made to serve the revolt of the masses. Furthermore, it had to construct a political and economic system that, while serving the particular interests of its rulers, must be identified with the higher interests of the entire nation. The organization of these tasks was to be the function of Fascism.

But the regime has one underlying reality. It is, as Mussolini has bluntly put it, 'a single police force.' [2] 'Our State,' he said, 'is a will to power and to domination.' [3] For Fascism, with all its elaborate structure and rationalization and mysticism, is merely a means for maintaining the power of a few men over the Italian people.

And means can become ends in themselves. The military and political interests of the Fascist hierarchy might finally prove fatal to the very social groups that called it to power.

When Mussolini became Prime Minister, in October 1922, he commanded but a handful of nominal followers in Parliament. For a moment it appeared that he might rule constitutionally, after all. He organized a coalition cabinet, which included not only Fascists and conservatives but even a Populist and a moderate Socialist. It was widely believed that the Fascist *coup* had not produced any fundamental political changes, and that soon the old parties would regain the upper hand. Veteran liberal politicians spoke confidently of the stable, energetic Government that must now bring peace and order to the country. The leaders of the General Confederation of Labor stood ready to collaborate with Mussolini. The conservative and moderate deputies meekly gave the new Government a vote of confidence. Thus the traditional forms were satisfied. But the political character of the new regime was soon made plain.

Mussolini had no intention of being held in check by the old parliamentary processes. He wished to govern with the consent of the people, he declared, but in any case govern he would. 'Force may produce consent, but even if consent is not forthcoming, there is still force.' [4] To this end, he took steps to make sure of his control of the agencies of coercion. The strength of the regular army was raised from 175,000 men to 275,000. Moreover, the Fascist punitive squads were regularized by the organization of a Blackshirt Militia of 190,000 men, sworn to the personal service of their Duce. This threatened not only the opposition, but also helped centralize command over the Fascist Party.

The Fascist leaders lost little time in rewarding the propertied men whose money had helped them to victory. Those elements in their program that had been borrowed from the Socialists were now forgotten. Indeed, they actually moved in the direction of *laissez-faire* at this time. Business men and landlords were released from annoyances to which they had recently been subjected. Capital issues were freed from taxation, the official commission of inquiry charged with discovering illicit war-profiteering was dissolved and its findings suppressed, and the family inheritance tax was abolished. Wherever possible, indirect taxes were substituted for direct.

The decrees that provided for cession of land to co-operatives were repealed, and peasants were ousted from estates that they had occupied. A proposed law for division of the *latifondi* was dropped, and the measures limiting rises in land rents and eviction of tenants were revoked. Financial support was withdrawn from the workers' co-operatives. Mussolini declared: 'I think that the State must renounce its economic functions, and above all those in the field of public utilities, because in this respect the State is incompetent.' [5] Most of the telephone system was handed over to private enterprise, and motions were even made to end State control of the railways, post offices, and telegraphs. The Government ceded its match-monopoly and its life-insurance business to private interests. The economic activities of municipalities were curtailed.

Such favors to the wealthy could not be granted without arousing conflict inside the Fascist ranks. The movement had attracted many people who were convinced that it stood for 'patriotic' political and economic reform in the interests of the middle and lower classes. Moreover, the Party had drawn to itself many blatant careerists, especially during 1921 and 1922. Once the Fascist leaders were installed in office, they tried to use their membership cards as a pass to spoils. This, too, was annoying to 'Fascists of the first hour.'

Dissension broke out within the Party—a conflict that, never becoming quite open, has continued to smoulder for many years, even suggesting at times a division into left- and right-wing groups. During 1923 Mussolini was obliged to hear bitter criticisms from many of his earliest and most zealous followers. Thus, in January 1923 a Fascist newspaper in Lombardy wrote: 'We must speak clearly. We cannot and must not forget that we were and still are Republicans. . . .

Fascism must be saved from prostitution.' [6] About the same time, another Fascist journal in Emilia declared: 'The landlords and industrialists are of the opinion that Fascism's purpose is to check the demands of labor, but not to resist exploitation by the capitalists. But two thousand Fascists did not die for this purpose, nor are two hundred thousand Fascists ready to die for this purpose.' [7] And a prominent Blackshirt [8] of the 'first hour' wrote in an open letter to Mussolini: 'I was a supporter of the first program of Fascism. . . . At that time you wore a red rosette over the tricolour in your buttonhole. But since then you have so changed the program of 1919 that now you are protecting the very people you promised to fight. You have thrown yourself into the arms of those whom you said you were going to destroy. And Fascism has identified itself with reaction in the service of the monarchy and bourgeoisie.' The Fascist leadership answered these attacks, and the attendant indiscipline among the rank and file, by 'purifying' and reorganizing the Party. Tens of thousands of old members were ousted, local Party groups were forbidden to concern themselves with national policies, new recruits were found among the bureaucracy. Finally, Party controls were centralized completely in the hands of the Duce and his immediate entourage.

Early in 1923 the old Nationalists merged with the Fascist Party. This was an important strengthening of the Fascist leadership. It won them the open support of many members of the nobility and upper middle class. It gave them the backing of monarchist, militarist, and conservative intellectual groups. Fascism thus became 'respectable.' The representatives of the privileges of big business, landed aristocracy, the army, and the Church, had captured a powerful position within the Fascist Party.

Yet dissident opinions, carefully veiled, continued in a portion of the Party. It was Mussolini's extraordinary political
talents that maintained a working balance. Indeed, an artful
juggling of contradictory elements among his followers—now
encouraging one group, then another—was vitally necessary
for the preservation of his personal power.

With control of the armed forces and the revenues of the
State in their hands, and with powerful vested interests re-
assured, the Fascists were in a position to destroy finally all
opposing forces within the country. The Blackshirt terror now
became systematic. Thousands of persons suspected of anti-
Fascist sentiments were persecuted and imprisoned.

But popular unrest mounted as the character of the new
regime became clearer. This was reflected in the growing circulation of opposition newspapers and an increasing restive-
ness in Parliament. The Catholic Populist members of Mussolini's cabinet resigned. A consolidation of Fascist political
power, based on a show of popular consent, was obviously de-
sirable. To this end a new electoral law—deliberately designed
to produce a majority for the Fascists—was bludgeoned
through Parliament, which thereupon was dissolved. The law
provided that the party which received one-fourth of the
votes cast was to obtain two-thirds of the seats in the Chamber. The Fascist press threatened that even if the election
went against the Party, it would remain in power. The election took place in April 1924. Inasmuch as the opposition
parties were prohibited from organizing their campaigns and
their supporters were intimidated, it is not surprising that the
Fascists, allied with their reactionary and conservative friends
in other parties, and heavily subsidized by the Association of
Italian Stock Companies, won their parliamentary majority.

Yet the new Parliament included a minority that continued

to criticize and protest. Giacomo Matteotti, a Socialist deputy, was especially outspoken in his denunciations of Fascist atrocities and electoral frauds. He paid for his courage with his life. The brutal kidnapping and murder of Matteotti by a gang of Blackshirts—who declared that they acted under the orders of Mussolini—rocked the country and brought to a head all the latent hostility to the regime. Everywhere, among all classes, angry voices were raised against the methods and policies of Fascism. For a moment its power seemed to be crumbling. The opposition parties—Socialists, Democrats, Catholics—withdrew in a body from Parliament. But they still could offer no more than a passive, rhetorical resistance. They yet hoped to reason with Fascism. Mussolini, at first taken aback by the storm of protest, soon recognized the continued impotence of his enemies. He recovered his balance and returned aggressively to the counter-attack. Provincial prefects were empowered to suppress opposition newspapers and curb the unions' activities. It was made plain to everyone that only the Fascist attitude would be tolerated.

Finally, on 3 January 1925, Mussolini declared bluntly to Parliament that he took upon himself complete responsibility for all that had occurred and challenged his enemies to oust him. The opposition was too timid and indecisive to take aggressive steps in its defense. It could do no more than draw up memoranda of protest. This date marks the beginning of the absolute dictatorship.

Mussolini's challenge set off a new and terrible onslaught on his enemies. Clubs and guns were too much for the righteous indignation of the anti-Fascists. Terrorism overwhelmed all opponents of the regime; thousands were killed, imprisoned, or exiled. A series of attempts on Mussolini's life served conveniently to establish laws suppressing his enemies. The vestiges of the old labor organizations collapsed, the Free-masons and other autonomous political parties and cultural societies were disbanded, critical journals were bought off or muzzled or destroyed. The civil service was purged of polit-ically suspect officials, whose posts were filled by loyal Fas-cists. Men who still dared to protest were beaten or terrified into silence. The forms of democratic government, and all the guarantees of personal rights that went with it, disappeared. The State became a ruthless censor of every form of public expression. Parliament was transformed into a mere conven-tion of the Party, without real authority. Actual law-making and enforcing powers were transferred to the Dictator. Local autonomy was abolished. An agreement between the Party and big industrial employers, providing for recognition of Fascist 'syndicates' as the sole labor organization, gave the final blow to the autonomous labor movement. The era of 'class-collaboration'—enforced by the Police Dictatorship—began.

Thus, by 1926 the fundamental reality of the Corporate State was established. The façade of liberal government was swept away, and there remained only the unhindered rule, sometimes gloved, sometimes naked, of force.

It was now possible to transform, without positive hin-drance, the basic social institutions in accordance with the spirit and practices of the ruling groups. Throughout the following years, the external forms of the Police State and its attempted justification were in process of elabora-tion.

The masses of the people, concerned with the day-to-day business of getting their living, submitted. They accepted Fascism, if not out of conviction, then out of stark necessity. And this, more than anything else, has made possible the con-tinued imposition of the Dictatorship. As the years have passed, the underlying masses have become publicly more and more unanimous and adulatory. Privately, as always in the past, they preserve their saving ability to mock their Caesars.

Central in the Fascist system is the concentration of powers in the 'Head of the Government.' In his hands are collected the controls over all ramifications of the political and economic structure. Every legislative and administrative action, every court decision, can be traced directly or indirectly back to his authority. In practice all laws are made by the Dictator and his ministers. Approval by an obedient parliament is always certain. He commands the military and police forces. Judges find it wise to accommodate their decisions to the 'general political direction of the Government.' All governmental posts are held at his pleasure. The Cabinet ministers have become his administrative assistants, responsible solely to him. And, lest any of his subordinates should become too powerful, Mussolini frequently 'changes the guard'—that is, potential rivals are abruptly dismissed, reduced in rank, or shifted to a more healthful climate. The most self-effacing officials are the ones who hold their posts longest. A series of laws have constitutionalized the absolute sovereignty of the Duce.

Yet it seems hardly possible that Mussolini alone has been responsible for the making of all major policies. Rather, it appears that he is essentially the *personification* of Dictatorship. Outwardly he is the inspired autocrat manipulating his puppets, and receiving credit for everything. In practice, however, rule is exercised collectively by a few leading administrators, including Mussolini, and their official and unofficial advisors. Their one basic and constant guiding principle is that their dominance be preserved.

A corollary of the development of absolute executive power has been the merging of the Fascist Party with the Government. Mussolini is at once the supreme leader of the Party and the head of the Government. He, together with his faithful hierarchs, controls the selection of Party functionaries, from highest to lowest, and governs all Party decisions. The Party's monopoly of thousands of jobs, and the special privileges given loyal Fascists in securing posts and winning promotions, are themselves a means of making members 'behave.' *

The Grand Council of Fascism has been elevated by law to the position of 'supreme organ co-ordinating all the activities of the regime.' It consists of outstanding Party dignitaries and of high officials of the political, military, cultural, and economic agencies. Presumably the Council is the 'supreme advisor' of Crown and Government, particularly in respect of constitutional law, questions of war and peace, and selection of cabinet ministers. But the Duce dominates the Grand Council, too, for he chooses its members, calls its meetings (always held secretly and in the blackest hours of the night), and is under no formal obligation to accept its advice.

Because its membership, both directly and through its associated bodies, penetrates every sphere of Italian society, the Party is an exceedingly valuable auxiliary of the regular Government in controlling the masses. It is defined, in fact, as a 'civil militia at the service of the Fascist State.' Each member must swear 'to obey the commands of the Duce . . . and when necessary to shed my blood for the Fascist Revolution.' The rank and file of the Party know little more of independent discussion and free choice of their officers than do non-

* The Party's membership at the end of 1937 totalled over two and a half millions. It included a considerable number of peasants and workers, but key posts were held predominantly by members of the upper and middle classes.

Fascists. And they have little opportunity to bring pressure on the Government. To be sure, if there is anything approaching political struggle in Fascist Italy, it is confined to the Party. But even there it is a conflict between outstanding personalities, temperaments, and ambitions, rather than a struggle over principles. Thus, it is hardly accurate to say that the body of Party membership is the 'governing *élite*' of the nation. The Party, rather, is one more obedient instrument of rule for the Dictator and the leading men of politics and property who surround him.

Until recently a vestige of the old Parliament lingered on. Members of the Chamber, nominally elective, in reality were chosen by the Government. Whenever it became expedient to select a new Chamber, the Fascist labor and employer associations nominated eight hundred candidates. An additional two hundred names were proposed by other Fascist organizations. (It goes without saying that all these nominations were 'guided' by the Fascist leaders.) From these thousand nominees the Grand Council might choose four hundred deputies, or it might select them elsewhere. The Grand Council's handpicked list then was presented to the voters, who were baldly asked to accept or reject it *in toto*. In the two elections held under this procedure—'pulp-paper revels,' Mussolini called them—the Government received almost unanimous approval. But inasmuch as the voters were subjected to immense pressure by the regime, there was really never the slightest possibility that the list would be rejected.

Thus the Chamber of Deputies became a debating club of Party politicians. Its meetings provided a sounding-board for statements on policy by the Duce and his ministers, and gave the faithful ample opportunities to make fawning speeches. For the deputies' addresses were mainly florid compliments to the Dictator. Occasionally, however, they did reflect differences of opinion within the upper ranks of the Party. With unimportant exceptions, the Chamber had no authority to initiate legislation; it was merely privileged to give rubber-stamp approval to measures prepared in ruling circles. But the Duce repeatedly announced that even this shell of parliament, this petrified symbol, must in time disappear.

Finally, in October 1938, the death warrant of the Chamber of Deputies—and of the vestiges of popular election of deputies—was signed by the Grand Council. Its place has been taken by a 'Chamber of Fasces and Corporations,' whose members are high Party functionaries and representatives of the economic 'Corporations.' The function of the new assembly is defined as 'collaboration with the Government in the formation of laws.' Its personnel and its actions are exclusively under the authority of the Duce. This time, the name of the orchestra was changed, but as before 'the music is always the same.'

The upper house of Parliament, the Senate, has remained unaltered in structure. But this convocation of elders never was a popular body. It was always a conservative forum of the high nobility and propertied gentry. As for the monarchy, its status is adequately mirrored in the doleful remark attributed to Victor Emmanuel during the days of the Ethiopian crisis: 'If Mussolini wins, I become Emperor of Ethiopia; if Mussolini loses, I shall at last become King of Italy.'

Furthermore, the provinces and municipalities have been brought completely under the heel of the central executive. Provincial government has been turned over to prefects, who act in accordance with instructions from Rome. For a time, certain local Fascist Party secretaries attempted to rival the prefects' authority. This was ended, at least formally, in 1927 when Mussolini ordered that the prefects were to be supreme within their jurisdictions in all except military and judicial matters. According to the Duce, 'Now that elections are no longer mentioned . . . the prefect must be at the head of the whole life of the province, and from the prefect the life of the province must receive its stimulus, co-ordination, and direction.' [9] In municipalities the *podestà*, another species of sub-dictator appointed by the central Government, has replaced the old elective mayors and town councils. Municipal advisory boards, nominated by local branches of the Fascist economic organs, might be consulted by the *podestà*, but he is not obliged to accept their suggestions.

Thus Fascism 'solemnly buried the lie of universal democratic suffrage.' Yet the Fascist Government has nevertheless been described by one of its admirers as 'a popular dictatorship because the powers have been conferred upon Mussolini by the popular will.' [10]

An elaborate network of police—civil, military, secret, and political—has been thrown over the country. In addition to the Fascist militia of nearly half a million men available for duty at a moment's notice, thousands of Blackshirts are kept on permanent service in guarding railways, posts and telegraphs, ports, frontiers, and the person of the Dictator. Outlays for internal policing have risen to a level ten times as great as before the World War. Rome is provided with a policeman for every seventy of its citizens. Close attention is paid to suspected anti-Fascists who, without trial before the regular courts, may be confined to their homes or communities or exiled to island concentration camps. A special military tribunal has been set up to try high offenses against the regime. A new and very reactionary penal code has been introduced. Described as providing 'energetic means for the defense of the State against the dangerous classes,' it is notable for its rigorous definition of crimes against the Dictatorship, the Monarchy, and the Church, and for the severity of its penalties in general. A dark shadow of terror, known and unknown, clouds the land.[11] Only a native kindliness and tolerance among the people saves them from the horrors implicit in the formalities of Fascist dictatorship.

The economic life of the country is also encased within the mold of dictatorship. A complex, State-controlled structure of monopolistic employer and labor associations, topped by 'Corporations,' gradually took shape after 1925. This so-called Corporate State, indeed, is said to be Fascism's most distinctive and significant social contribution. Its ostensible purpose was to inaugurate the happy reign of class-collaboration, superseding the tumult of class-struggle and the confusions of economic individualism. A Fascist commentator has said: 'The agnosticism of the liberal State in the face of economic and social conflicts has been superseded by a chain of well-harmonized institutions . . . in which the principle of State supremacy is completed by that of perfect equality between capital and labor. . . .' [12]

As already stated, the Fascists had made vigorous efforts from the first to organize their own occupational unions in order to weaken the Socialists and Catholics. During 1920–23, while the 'red' organizations were declining, the Fascist labor and employer associations became increasingly powerful. Thanks to the Blackshirt terror, the old unions were destroyed, leaving the Fascist 'syndicates' alone in the labor field. On the other hand, the old associations of landlords and industrialists were the nucleus around which the Fascist employers' syndicates formed. For a time there was resistance by the big industrialists to their submergence in State organizations. The Fascist 'labor leaders' replied by calling a number of strikes. Finally, in 1925, an agreement between the Government and the General Confederation of Industry gave the Fascist syndicates a complete monopoly in representing labor. At the same time, the General Confederation was recognized as the sole representative of industrial employers. Furthermore, the workers' shop councils—so annoying to the industrialists—were abolished.

It now remained to give legal effect to what had been accomplished: conversion of the labor organizations into submissive creatures of the Government. This was substantially achieved in 1926, when parallel bodies of workers and employers—the former, at any rate, entirely under governmental control—were set up for each trade or occupation. Only one union (the Fascist syndicate, of course) in each occupational group is 'legally' recognized as the exclusive representative of all the workers or employers, whether union members or not.[13] All other associations are in practice prohibited. Nonmembers are required to pay the same dues as members. The worker-members can take no active part in the functioning of their unions. Syndicate officials are in effect named by and responsible solely to the Government. Local unions of workers in each single trade are grouped in federations, and, in turn, the federations representing broad branches of the economy are united in 'confederations.' * The employers' syndical associations are similarly organized.

---

* One each for industry, agriculture, commerce, credit and insurance, and the liberal professions. For several years all the labor syndicates were joined together in a single nation-wide confederation. In 1928, however, six *separate* confederations were established, thus splitting the body of labor into distinct compartments. This represented a set-back for certain 'labor-minded' Fascists—notably Edmondo Rossoni—who, with a unified labor organization at their command, might well have challenged Mussolini.

The chief function of the parallel syndicates is the making of collective labor contracts, specifying wage-rates, hours, and other aspects of the job. The contracts supposedly express 'the conciliation of labor and employer interests and their subordination to the higher interests of production.' Their provisions, when ratified by the Government, are binding on all employers and workers (whether syndicate-members or not) of the trades specified. That is, the Government with the assistance of the bigger employers defines the conditions of labor. The syndicates are also required to represent the employers and workers before the courts, to supervise social-welfare schemes, and to collaborate with the Government in carrying out its economic programs. In addition, they act as propaganda agents for the 'corporative philosophy.'

All forms of independent action on the part of the workers—such as the boycott and strike—are illegal. And the law, in its avowed impartiality, also forbids lockouts. Disputes between workers and employers may be settled by mediation on the part of the syndical officials. If that proves fruitless, then recourse can be taken to 'Courts of Labor,' whose sentence is final. In either case, it is the omnipotent Government that decides.

With the establishment of the syndicates, in 1926, Mussolini announced that the Corporate State had come into being: 'We are . . . a State which controls all forces acting in nature. We control political forces, we control material forces, we control economic forces, therefore we are a full-blown Corporate State.' [14]

Supreme administrative authority over the entire syndical structure is exercised by a Ministry of Corporations (successor to the old ministries of national economy and labor), which of course is directly under the control of the Dictator. Provincial Councils of Corporations have been set up to 'represent in a unitary and integral manner the interests of the economic activities of their respective provinces, and assure and promote their co-ordination and development in harmony with the general interests of the nation.' Their members represent the syndicates and various governmental economic bodies. Substantially, these Councils are the local chambers of commerce recast in the Fascist pattern. Other 'corporative' institutions have likewise been created by the simple process of giving new names to existing organizations. In 1930 it was decided to go a step farther in the making of the Corporate State, which up to that time had amounted to little more than a substitution of the controlled syndicates for the old autonomous labor unions. With much fanfare a National Council of Corporations was brought into being. It too was made up of Government officials and representatives of employers' and workers' syndicates (chosen of course by the Government). Although described by Mussolini as 'the thinking brain which prepares and co-ordinates' [15] economic policy, the National Council remained merely an advisory and speech-making body, concerned with wholly minor issues.

But the Corporate State was not yet completed.* An impatient Fascist deputy pointed out in 1932: 'We are still getting ready for the Corporative State. The minister, indeed, has told us several times that we were rapidly nearing the Corporative State. But we cannot say that we have quite reached it.' [16] At last, in November 1933, Mussolini proclaimed: 'To-day we are burying economic liberalism. . . .

---

* It must be emphasized that the corporative structure was not built in all its parts as one complete system. Its development has been frankly opportunistic. Some of its elements have disappeared as quickly as they have arrived. Others have no more meaning than windows painted on blank walls.

To-day we are taking another step forward on the road of the Revolution. . . . A revolution in order to be great must be a social revolution.' [17]

The 'revolutionary step' to which the Duce referred was the creation, at long last, of Fascist 'Corporations.' These bodies, twenty-two in number, also were to represent in an 'integral, national form' the various branches of the economy.[18] Each Corporation comprises a particular 'productive cycle,' consisting of producers of raw materials, processors, and distributors. For example, the 'cereals Corporation' includes employers and employees engaged in wheat farming, milling, baking, selling bread, and the like. At the head of each Corporation is a council, consisting of delegates of the Fascist Party, representatives of the employers' and workers' syndicates in the fields comprised by the Corporation, and technical experts.* Again, all are appointed, directly or indirectly, by the Government. The employers' delegation includes most of the important men of big business affairs, while the employees are represented largely by reliable accountants, engineers, professors, lawyers, doctors, and politicians. Hardly any delegates come from the rank and file of workers. That is, the councils consist of employers and Party officials chosen by other Party officials.

The Corporations are authorized to advise the Government on economic problems, to conciliate labor disputes, determine wages, and formulate 'rules regarding economic relations and the discipline of production.' Inasmuch as the Government can always choose to accept or ignore their recommendations, these powers are more apparent than real. A Central Corporative Committee, composed of certain cabinet ministers, Party leaders, and high officials of the Corporations and syndical

---

* The Party delegates are supposed to represent consumers and the nation as a whole.

confederations, appears to be the only authoritatively significant body in the formal economic structure. Still, it was promised that the functions and powers of the Corporations would in time be increased. And the Duce more than once announced that their councils must eventually take the place of the Chamber of Deputies. By moving slowly, the Fascists have maintained their 'permanent revolution.' Thus have they been 'teaching the people bit by bit to govern themselves.' [19]

The spirit of 'corporativism' and the putative principles governing capital and labor relationships were laid down in a 'Charter of Labor' (1927). This collection of vague aphorisms was hailed as the fundamental statute of the corporate regime. Professional Fascists described it as 'a document without precedent in constitutional history.' [20] Its phrases roll out magnificently: 'The Italian Nation is an organism endowed with purposes, a life, and means of action transcending in power and duration those of the individuals, singly or grouped, that compose it. . . . Labor in all its forms . . . is a social duty, and only because of this it is protected by the State. . . . The mass of production is a unit from the National point of view; it has a single object, namely, the well-being of individuals and the development of national power. . . . Solidarity between the various factors of production is concretely expressed by the Collective Labor Contract, which conciliates the opposing interests of employers and workers, subordinating them to the higher interests of production. . . .' Thus the Charter emphasizes the admirable concept that economic life is subordinate to the interests of the entire community, in whose name and under whose guidance capital and labor must collaborate. But its words are ambiguous, explaining nothing. On the contrary, they are themselves in need of explanation.

The Charter at least gives a sonorously formal voice to some of the economic pretensions of Fascism. Moreover, its 'guarantees' of the social supremacy, the duties and rights, of labor are a ritualistic consolation to the Italian proletariat. At times, Fascism has appeared more socialistic than Socialism. 'Fascism is not opposed to Socialism in itself,' it has been said, 'but only to the theoretical and practical degeneration of Socialism.' [21] A legion of Fascist professors has set to work on long-winded commentaries on the philosophy and practice of corporativism. Unfortunately, as one of their number has gloomily admitted, 'the same ideas expressed by Mussolini, when repeated by others, whether commentators or interpreters, lose all their tonality and seducing beauty.' [22] Their writings about economic life under the new order dilate on Fascist 'principles,' the 'social duties' of employers, the 'corporate conscience,' 'class-collaboration,' conversion of workers into 'true producers'—invariably interlarded with extravagant homage to the Duce—but have little to tell about underlying realities. A new nomenclature has been invented: private property = 'National Wealth'; employers and workers = 'Producers'; employer-Fascist domination = 'Class-collaboration'; terrorization of opponents = 'National Discipline'; wage cuts and taxes = 'Patriotic Sacrifices.' The 'corporate' language is soothing but uncertain. For example: 'Corporate action is a great spiritual function. It gives a new spiritual status to the producer, lends a new significance to his work. His point of view changes, his work assumes a new value, becomes a public function. . . . The true corporate action is born and is developing from a spiritual need: it is an action in which the individual's profit-motive is one of the minor factors and often a handicap. The corporate attitude and spirit is that of the future man. [And so on.]'[23] The academicians' smoke-screen of words all too often hides the real Italy from the gaze of outsiders. For the meaning of the bureaucracy known as the Corporate State is to be found—not in the vapors of Fascist ideology—but only in the daily lives of the people themselves.

Fundamental in making the totalitarian State is the effort to conquer the rational and—far more important—the irrational mind of the masses. They must develop a slavish attitude that automatically indentifies the Fascist State with the realization of their own ambitions. Externally, at least, the regime has gone far towards this goal. Every conceivable mode of expression is captured and prostituted to the cultivation of a mythology of Mussolini and Fascism. Most important are rigid control of the press, exploitation of the youth, and a working alliance with the Church. In all the arts of persuasion the Fascist leaders have shown remarkable ingenuity. The content of their propaganda is suited to the emotional mass-mind; its technique revolves around the use of suggestive symbols and catch-phrases, ceremonial regalia, spectacular assemblages, warlike theatrics. Injecting color where before there was drabness, playing on the fears and hopes of common men, Fascism has forged a powerful weapon of rule.

The press has become a grovelling servant of the Government. Provincial prefects are given extensive powers of censorship. Every newspaper must have a 'responsible' (that is, a fascistic) editor, and only journalists congenial to the Government may be employed. A Ministry of Propaganda undertakes to color important despatches and to dole out instructions on the treatment of news items. Not all publications are formal organs of the Party, but unswerving obedience is a *sine qua non* for their existence. Certainly an occasional feeble and minor criticism is not considered incompatible with such fealty. But on all basic issues there can be only one language. In consequence, Italian newspapers have descended to a ridiculously phonographic level, monotonous and uniform. All arrogance and bombast, they vapidly sing the triumphs of Mussolini and the glories of Fascism. To learn what is taking place in the world, educated Italians eagerly seize upon such foreign newspapers as they can get. Yet Mussolini has said: 'Journalism is free just because it serves only one cause and one regime.' [24]

Likewise, educational institutions—from primary school to university—have been 'fascisticized.' That is, they have become agencies for making the youth blindly obedient and for depriving them of desire to think for themselves. Suspected anti-Fascists are weeded out of the teaching ranks. Textbooks are carefully concocted doses of propaganda. The whole educational process is set in the pattern of an extravagant chauvinism. 'Believe, obey, fight!', (meaning: 'Do not reason, give up your personality, ask no questions!') is the maxim of the schools. The children learn that 'just as religious dogmas are not discussed because they are truths revealed by God, so Fascist principles are not to be discussed because they emanate from the mind of a genius—Benito Mussolini.'[25] They are told, 'Remember to love God, but do not forget that the God of Italy is the Duce.' Before their mid-day meal, taken in school, they repeat a grace: 'Duce, I thank You for what You give me to make me grow healthy and strong. O Lord God, protect the Duce so that He may be long preserved to Fascist Italy.' [26]

The Government has also established extra-curricular organizations to provide for further physical, military, and patriotic education of children from the ages of six to eighteen. These have undoubtedly done much towards improving the physical health of the younger generation. Thoroughly war-like in character, they probably are much more significant than the schools in inspiring the young people with devotion to Fascism. Recruits for the Party are drawn from the graduating classes of the youth organizations. Therefore membership is practically obligatory for the sake of future security, even if it is not attractive for its own sake.

Early Fascism displayed an extreme anti-clerical bias. Catholic political and labor organizations were shown little more mercy than the Socialist under the attacks of the Blackshirts. But from the beginning, too, many Fascists (particularly the men of the old Nationalist Party) recognized that the Church, with its following among the humble masses, could be of great value in buttressing their regime. Despite interludes of bitter hostility, a rapprochement was gradually achieved. In 1929, the Lateran Treaty restored, at least formally, the temporal sovereignty of the Papacy. The Government gave the Holy See a very substantial indemnity (1,750 million lire in cash and bonds) for the occupation of Rome in 1870. Religious marriage was introduced and religious instruction became obligatory in the secondary schools. Other concessions enlarged the influence of the Church over family life and education. However, the Church was required to limit its propaganda to matters of religion, and to abstain from competing with the Fascist youth movement. Mussolini warned: 'Catholicism completes Fascism, and this we openly declare, but let no one think they can turn the tables on us, under cover of metaphysics or philosophy.'[27] Thus the Duce, who years before had written scurrilous defamations of the Church and its works, became Pius XI's 'Man of Providence.'

The Church soon discovered that it had fallen, however unwillingly, into a *de facto* alliance with the Dictatorship. The capitulation of the Italian clergy to the seductions of Fascism has been almost complete. Occasional disputes arise, but there appears to be no will to press them far. Early in 1937, the Cardinal-Archbishop of Milan compared the Duce with the glorious Roman emperors, and sent his greetings 'to the Italian legions which occupy Ethiopia in order to assure that people the double advantage of imperial civilization and the Catholic faith.' [28] The fate of the Italian Church seems irrevocably bound up with Fascism.

Fascism has filled the vessels of propaganda with its own mysteries. Possessing little independent rational strength, the movement tries to drown the reality of its origin and nature in a flood of words. 'If Fascism does not wish to die or, worse still, to commit suicide,' wrote Mussolini to an associate in 1921, 'it must now provide itself with a doctrine. Yet this shall not and must not be a robe of Nessus clinging to us for all eternity, for tomorrow is something mysterious and unforeseen. . . . I do wish that during the two months which are still to elapse before our National Assembly meets, the philosophy of Fascism could be created.' [29] Thanks to the labors of its host of intellectual paramours, Fascism was not long embarrassed by the lack of a philosophy. At times, indeed, it even seemed to suffer from having too many contradictory doctrinal fragments left on its door-step. For its rationale has been compounded of many different ideas whose only qualification is that they should envelop the regime in respectability and help to draw attention away from stark realities. Mussolini has frankly said: 'I do not take much stock in these ideals, but I do not exclude them because I exclude nothing.' [30] All that needed exclusion were intellectual currents which made for skepticism. Machiavelli, Hobbes, Hegel, Gioberti, Nietzsche, Sorel, Pareto, D'Annunzio (perhaps even an unnamed Socialist philosopher or two) have been seized upon to make their due contributions. 'We allow ourselves,' Mussolini has said, 'the luxury of being aristocrats and democrats; conservatives and progressives; reactionaries and revolutionaries; legitimists and illegitimists, according to conditions of time, place, and circumstance.' Unscrupulous, certainly, but also effective politics. Fascism has the great merit of meaning different things to different minds, thus enabling every man—if he wishes—to find sufficient reason for his allegiance to the regime.

To some, Fascism has been a revival of the Roman *cultus*, and Mussolini nothing less than a reborn Caesar Augustus. The Duce, indeed, encourages such comparisons. Legends and monuments of ancient Rome have been hauled out of their débris and exhibited as proper background for the latter-day Imperator. In Mussolini's vocabulary, the word 'Roman' tends to take the place of 'Italian.'

Again, Fascism has been described as a 'rural phenomenon,' guiding Italy back to the virtues of the simple life. Another version—attractive to 'bolshevistic' Blackshirts—presents Fascism as the Italian form of proletarian revolution, inaugurating the era of 'the power and glory of Labor.' Fascism can even be seen as a Christian revival: 'The Kingdom of Love must be established in spirit as well as in matter. That is the great teaching of Fascism.'[31] And again, 'It is . . . only in the Fascist climate that the law of Christ, the law of love for the little child, can be carried out.' [32]

In every mood, however, there is deification of Mussolini and worship of that powerful abstraction, the National State. The Fascist State must be all-inclusive, omnipotent—'everything in the State, nothing against the State, nothing outside the State.' [33] And the State must be adored at the shrine of the infallible and heaven-sent Duce, the supreme inspirer and creator, from whom all good things descend upon ordinary men.

In this atmosphere, material standards are presumed to mean nothing. Mussolini has proclaimed: 'If it be true that matter was on the altars for one century, to-day it is the spirit that takes its place. . . . By saying that God is returning, we mean that spiritual values are returning.' [34] The sacred fundamentals of Fascism may not be discussed; they must be accepted in ecstatic faith. 'Fascism,' it is insisted, 'should be interpreted with the same criterion used for phenomena of a religious and moral nature . . .' [35] Nevertheless, because the vulgar notions of another century still persist among the Italians, Fascism cannot escape altogether from the need to justify itself in terms of the people's material wants.

The Fascist mythos undoubtedly has captured the imagination and loyalty of great numbers of Italians. Much of the youth has been converted, earnestly and even passionately, by the black mass of Fascism. Others perhaps have found a refuge from the uncertainties and insecurities of the post-war world in the idea of omniscient dictatorship. But from another and perhaps larger number of people Fascism has been unable to extract more than lip service. (Yet that is probably enough for purposes of rule.) The Police State has erected an imposing façade. Can it also build itself an enduring foundation?

# IV : WORKERS OF FIELD AND FACTORY

ACCORDING to the Fascists, the central factor in the alleged social breakdown of post-war Italy was the bitter strife between selfish groups of capitalists and laborers. They argue that Fascism brought domestic peace and stability, not by crushing one side or the other, but by substituting 'class-collaboration' for the old class-struggle. Mussolini's words are: 'I proclaim, with my armed militia at my right and my judges at my left, that from now on capital and labor will have equal rights and equal duties, and will be brothers in the Fascist family.' [1] The Charter of Labor expresses this idea more formally. It describes 'work in all its forms—intellectual, technical, manual, organizing, or executive—as a social duty,' and 'private enterprise in the field of production as the most effective and efficient means and the one most consonant with national interests,' and it states that 'production is a matter of national concern and, therefore, the organizer of business is responsible to the State for the direction given thereto.' However, it adds that the 'syndicates legally recognized and subject to State control alone have the right of legal representation of the whole category of employees and workers for which they are constituted.'

The Fascist ideal of 'class-collaboration' in the field of capital and labor relations is to be attained mainly by the syndicate system. The syndical machinery, it is claimed, must 'eliminate once and for all the use of violent methods' in the settlement of disputes between employer and employee. In this way the Fascist 'authoritarian democracy' is to be achieved.

75

According to Mussolini, 'Fascism establishes the real equality of individuals before labor and before the nation. . . . The object of the regime in the economic field is to ensure higher social justice for the whole Italian people. What does higher social justice mean? It means security of the job, fair wages, a comfortable home. It means the possibility of continuous evolution and improvement. Nor is this enough. It means that the workers must enter more and more intimately into the productive process and share its necessary discipline.' [2] Thus the Duce himself lays down the test of Fascism's system of 'class-collaboration.' Does the system stand up under this test?

It is clear that the monopolistic employers' and workers' syndicates do not operate democratically. The employers' associations appear to be dominated by a few of the more influential men of big business and by Party leaders. And the labor syndicates are but plastic creatures of the Fascist State. According to Mussolini, 'the Fascist syndicates form a great mass completely under the control of Fascism and the Government: a mass that obeys.' [3] But because of close personal relationships between the more important employers and the Fascist hierarchy, this control weighs most heavily on the labor organizations. A labor court has held that 'the syndicates are State organs, and not organizations of the working class; they are dependent upon the State.' [4]

Certainly the labor syndicates have nothing in common with trade unions elsewhere except a similarity in form. Not all workers are required to join the syndicates, to be sure, but all of them—members and non-members alike—have to pay dues, and all are subject to the working conditions specified in the official collective contracts. The syndical officers are in no way dependent upon the worker-members for their positions—no more than generals owe their posts to the common soldiers of their armies. Formally, it is true, the lowest grades of functionaries are 'elected' by the syndicate members. Yet it is admitted that the 'elections' are merely routine and foregone approvals of choices made in higher quarters. A syndical leader has frankly explained to an American investigator: 'We send an official to hold the local meeting. He suggests a person whom we think suitable to be their secretary. That person is usually elected without question. There may sometimes be some boos and groans. In that case we talk it over with them.' [5] The Fascist point of view is that 'the elections are only an administrative matter: the means that enable the masses to affirm their loyalty to the Government by voting for men who are *persona grata*.' [6] In effect, then, the subordinates are appointed to their posts by superior officials. The latter in turn are responsible only to still higher officials (not only those of the Ministry of Corporations, but also those of the Ministry of Interior and of the Party), culminating finally in the authority of the Dictator.

As for the character of the syndical officers, according to Edmondo Rossoni, they 'should remain what they are: Blackshirts appointed by the Government to direct the syndicates.' [7] Only minor posts in the labor syndicates are filled by men coming from the employees' ranks. The superior officials and their employed staffs are overwhelmingly of middle-class origins, and consider themselves equivalent to civil servants. They have to give proof of 'national faith'—that is to say, they must be unquestioningly loyal, not necessarily to their worker constituents, but to the Fascist regime. On the other hand, most of the elected officials of the employers' syndicates are connected with the enterprises they represent.

It is these syndical functionaries who are charged with

drafting the terms of collective labor contracts (that is, the 'agreements' between masters and men which fix the nominal conditions of employment). Negotiations leading up to the conclusion of such contracts are carried on solely by the officials of employers' and employees' syndicates—in other words, by representatives of business interests and of the ruling bureaucracy. The workers' function is to accept and obey. To avoid any danger of carrying on negotiations in an atmosphere that might somehow be influenced by the wishes of the employees, it is provided that a contract may not go into effect until approved by the Ministry of Corporations, nor may it be made on any narrower regional basis than that of an entire province. In effect, it is the Government that makes the contract.

Fascist propagandists are fond of citing the large number of collective employer-labor contracts that have from time to time been put into effect. Thus, the 17,000-odd agreements concluded by the end of 1937 were hailed as evidence of the healthy functioning of the Corporate State. Although collective labor contracts in Italy antedated the World War, Fascist spokesmen sometimes claim for their regime the honor of having invented this method of defining conditions of work. As a rule, however, they are less inclined to discuss the actual contents of the Fascist labor agreements. And, of course, it is not the number of contracts, but the hours of work specified, the wages, the security of employment that really matter.

Obviously, in such a system of labor unions the role of the workers is simply to pay their dues and obey. The voices of the rank and file find no expression, unless it is to recite the words of thanks and praise for the Duce that their leaders periodically require of them. In consequence, from the standpoint of the workers the syndicates are sterile. Meetings are held infrequently, and then mainly to hear eulogistic speeches by officials. The mass of the members remains passive. But they cannot do otherwise. All independent discussion and criticism is denied them.* To strike or boycott, even for the purpose of enforcing the official labor contracts, is to commit a crime against the State. Strikes take place, nevertheless, under the Fascist 'labor peace.' (During 1926–34 there were 165 strikes; the number of workers involved, however, was only a few thousand. Since then, strikes and lockouts have been officially reported as 'crimes against the public economy.' Such crimes numbered 93 in 1935–6.) One can only wonder at the courage—or is it ignorance?—of those who dare to defy the regime. As long ago as 1929 an American observer reported: 'Labor organizations having been built into the state, strikers are promptly jailed. The labor problem in Italy no longer exists.' [8]

Of course, lockouts as well as strikes are declared illegal. Thus the equality of the law is preserved for rich and poor alike. Yet if an employer closes his plant on the ground that he cannot operate under existing wage conditions, his action might be viewed as 'justifiable.' 'Class-collaboration' is like the collaboration of horse and rider.

What of the 'higher social justice,' the guaranteed work, fair wages, decent homes, which Mussolini holds forth as the constant goal of his regime?

The Charter of Labor reintroduced the concept of the 'just wage.' It promises that wages should 'correspond to the normal requirements of life, the possibilities of production, and the output of labor. Wages shall be determined without

* In 1934 the Government introduced a worker's passport, the *libretto di lavoro*. This records the personal history of the worker, and shows whether his conduct is 'satisfactory from the National [i.e., the Fascist] standpoint.'

reference to any general rules, by agreement between the parties to the collective contracts.' That is, there can be no legal guarantee of minimum wages.

The elegant phrases of the Charter had scarcely ceased echoing in the Italian press when a major offensive on wage rates began. Indeed, it may not have been an accident that the Charter was promulgated on the eve of this attack. Perhaps the mysticism of 'higher national interest,' 'nobility of labor,' 'social duty of property,' was meant to reconcile the workers to the rude reality of wage cuts.

Real wages had been falling already in 1925 and 1926—that is, during a time of business prosperity, but also a time in which the defenses of the old labor unions had been shattered. Again, in the spring of 1927 'spontaneous' cuts took place. But towards the end of the year, with the stabilization of the lira, the Government began to intervene vigorously in order to force down the entire level of money wages. In October 1927 reductions of 10 per cent were imposed. Despite assurances by Mussolini that further cuts would not be permitted, the decline continued. According to Bruno Biagi, who for some time held the authoritative post of Under-Secretary of Corporations, 'from June 1927 to December 1928 wages fell about 20 per cent; there was a further reduction of 10 per cent in 1929, and in November 1930 there was a general decline, in some cases not exceeding 18 per cent but in other cases reaching 25 per cent. Many other adjustments were made in 1931.' [9] And, it should be pointed out, further 'adjustments' took place thereafter. By 1934 the money wages of industrial employees on an average probably had fallen at least 30 to 40 per cent below the level of 1926. Agricultural-workers' wages dropped quite as precipitously. According to official statistics, the average wages of male farm laborers throughout the country declined from 14 lire per day in 1927 to 8.90 lire in 1935—a reduction of 37 per cent in eight years. In individual provinces and trades the cuts varied considerably (roughly from 20 to 60 per cent), but in every instance they were serious. One of the functions of the syndical officials in this period was to induce employees to accept their wage reductions without too much grumbling. Thanks to Fascist syndicalism, labor expenses became the conveniently elastic item in production costs of Italian industry.

In the meantime, the Government sought to bring down the cost of living. But this effort was less fruitful than the wage-cutting campaign. Living costs fell by about 25 per cent between 1927 and 1934. That is, average real-wage rates declined 15 to 20 per cent during these years. If the reduction during 1925–6 is also taken into account, it appears that by 1935 the purchasing power of hourly or daily wages had shrunk to roughly four-fifths of what it had been about the time of Fascism's rise to power. Some officials even admitted that wages in particular trades had fallen to levels lower than those prevailing on the eve of the World War.

In short, much of the gains in wage rates won by organized labor during and immediately after the war were wiped out under Fascism. Yet some eminent persons have considered the decline in wages most healthful to the minds of the workers. For example, Signor Bottai discovered that lower wages 'would have valuable psychological and moral consequences by enforcing a more rigorous mode of living.' [10]

With the beginning of the Abyssinian War, the downward movement of wages stopped. Rapidly rising costs of living led to advances of wage rates during 1936 and 1937. Yet this has not compensated for higher living costs: wage increases totalled 18 to 25 per cent, but the cost of living rose at least 30 per cent from the end of 1934 to early 1938.[11]

It should be noted, moreover, that these observations relate only to contractual hourly or daily wage rates. A law of 1923 supposedly limited the normal working hours in all occupations to eight a day or 48 a week. Yet this law was so qualified that employers, especially in agriculture, may prolong the working day beyond the nominal limit without being bound to pay overtime wages. Thus, during the summer months—when work is at its heaviest and the only time when some workers can find employment—laborers may be required to work ten hours a day without extra compensation. Also, violations of the wage and hours provisions of labor contracts are very numerous. Evidence of this is to be found in the many complaints made by individual workers to the syndical authorities, and in guarded comments in the press. For example, 'labor' newspapers pointed out that workers 'are obliged by the scarcity of jobs to compete with one another to the extent of making contract terms almost meaningless,' that 'violations continue all along the line,' and that 'the majority of employers do not respect the wages set in the contracts.' [12] The journal of the farm-workers' confederation also lamented that 'we certainly have the right to ask that the nominal wage rates be respected by the people who have agreed to them, now that the field-workers have seen their wages reduced fifty per cent.' [13] An industrial employer and Party member suggested that the remedy for such violations was to cut wages further: 'It is necessary that the minimum wage be low enough to avoid the inevitable and unfortunately widespread violations.'

In examining workers' incomes, account must also be taken of the great increase in unemployment and partial unemployment during the years when wage rates were rapidly falling. In 1925 and 1926—when industrial activity was high and emigration outlets were still open—the number of jobless workers ranged between 80,000 and 200,000. But with the development of the economic crisis unemployment mounted alarmingly. In February 1932 the number of officially registered unemployed was 1,148,000; by February 1933 it was 1,225,000; it was still over a million in the winters of 1933–4 and 1934–5. Even in the seasonally active summer months of 1932–4 it ranged between 800,000 and 900,000. And the official figures certainly underestimate the actual unemployment. Probably as much as a fifth of all wage workers were jobless during the worst periods of these years. Most seriously affected were the industrial employees of Piedmont and Lombardy, and the farm laborers of Venetia and Emilia. Men and women who were able to hold their jobs, even though at reduced wages, were fortunate.

The meager relief afforded by unemployment insurance was quite inadequate to meet the mounting needs of the jobless. A compulsory unemployment-insurance system was established three years before the March on Rome. However, certain classes of employees might not be insured, most notably the three million domestic and farm laborers. (Agricultural workers were entitled to unemployment benefits under the original legislation, but the Fascist regime excluded them.) The insured unemployed received very small payments—1.25 to 3.75 lire a day—and then for only 90 days. At no time, apparently, did more than a quarter of the unemployed receive even these pittances.

The Government therefore had to adopt other devices for unemployment-relief. It tried to encourage seasonal migration of farm laborers to regions where they could be given at least temporary jobs. It also fell back on the old Socialist 'tax in workers' which obliged agricultural employers to hire a minimum number of laborers per acre under cultivation. At the same time, efforts were made to reduce the number of casual farm workers by extending the share-cropper system. The widely advertised settlement of peasants and rural workers on reclaimed land and in the colonies proved to be of little help. Emigration—by far the most important outlet for the more wretched workers and peasants in earlier years—had become only a minor palliative because of barriers raised abroad. But the Fascist Government itself had taken drastic steps to curb emigration at a time when opportunities were still available. When—faced by the rising tide of unemployment— it attempted to encourage at least seasonal migration of workers, the doors of neighboring countries were closed. The decline of emigration also meant a great shrinkage in the savings sent home by Italians abroad, savings that previously had played so important a part in improving living conditions in South Italy.

To relieve industrial unemployment, efforts were made to reduce working hours. The forty-hour week was established in industrial enterprises by agreement in October 1934 between the confederations of industrial workers and employers. This took place, it must be observed, only after employment had declined seriously and after many firms were already working less than forty hours a week. Although this measure resulted in the part-time re-employment of some 130,000 men, it was simply a work-sharing program. Earnings were reduced in proportion to the cut in working-hours. Thus, the workers again were obliged to shoulder the burdens of unemployment. Attempts were also made to eliminate women employees and to prevent the introduction of labor-saving machinery.

More significant was an expanded public-works program. Government outlays for road and railway-making, land reclamation, construction of public buildings, monuments, and the like, averaged about 2,000 million lire a year during 1930–36. This program, although given much publicity as another example of ingenious and novel Fascist 'planning,' absorbed not more than 15 to 20 per cent of all unemployed workers. Distress among the unemployed was also slightly relieved through the distribution of funds in deeply depressed areas by the Fascist Party and syndical organizations. The funds for such assistance came in large part from levies on employers and employees, although it was Mussolini who usually received personal credit.

Mention must also be made of the statistical onslaught on unemployment. For example, it appears that unemployed women workers at times were excluded from the register. Municipal officials were authorized to expel from the towns and send back to their native villages all jobless persons who had no early prospects of finding work. In 1933 new criteria of unemployment were adopted for the purpose of excluding other groups of unemployed from the statistics.

Ultimately, war and preparation for war have proved to be the most important deliberate means of reducing unemployment. The marked rise in the number of persons hired during 1935 is undoubtedly in large part attributable to mobilization for the war on Abyssinia. During 1935 and 1936 re-employment received considerable stimulus from the boom in war industries promoted by the Government, as well as from economic recovery elsewhere in the world. Unfortunately, unemployment statistics have not been published since 1935. However, it is estimated that in 1937 the total number of man-hours of employment in industry had risen to about

90 per cent of the 1928 level, and that the number of workers employed was nearly 5 per cent greater than in 1928. It is possible, then, that real incomes of many workers improved during 1936–7.

It might be said, in defense of the Fascist regime, that it is not *per se* responsible for the growth of unemployment on such an enormous scale. (To this one might reply that the regime, at any rate, has prolonged an economic system that operates at high human cost.) Moreover, the apologists of Fascism assert that after 1922 the Italian working masses received the benefits of greatly increased social services—services that did not appear in wage incomes but nevertheless contributed substantially to raising the workers' standard of living. Mussolini boasts that 'in the field of social legislation Italy leads the vanguard of all the nations.' [14]

Formally, indeed, the organization of social services is impressive. All workers are entitled to insurance benefits in the event of industrial diseases and accidents, to old-age and invalidity pensions, and to insurance against tuberculosis. A substantial number are insured against unemployment. Small supplements to the wages of laborers with large families have also been introduced. Women workers are entitled to maternity benefits. Voluntary sickness funds have been set up by business firms and the syndical organizations. Furthermore, the Government has fostered a number of social-welfare institutions. The most important of these is the *Dopolavoro*, or Leisure-Time Institute, which provides it members with admirable opportunities for education, sport, and recreation. By 1938 it had more than 3,000,000 members. Fascist youth, maternity, and infancy organizations are said also to have made material additions to the well-being of workers.

The promotion of these services is a striking contrast to

Mussolini's promise in September 1922 that he would 'wipe out the entire superstructure of the State.' [15] After all, most of the social services were established before the March on Rome. A beginning was made with industrial-accident insurance as far back as 1884; in 1904 it became compulsory for industrial workers, and in 1917 for agricultural workers. General unemployment insurance and old-age and invalidity pensions were initiated in 1919. Tuberculosis insurance was introduced by the Fascist Government in 1929, but much work like that of the Fascist social-welfare organizations was done by the old labor unions and other bodies. In fact, it was the growing pressure of politically organized labor that led to the adoption of social legislation. Similarly, labor exchanges, annual paid vacations, and a law requiring Sunday rest, were all known to pre-Fascist Italy. For one reason or another, the Fascists have seen fit to retain these heritages from the old regime, to expand them in certain directions, and to claim them as their own invention.

Closer observation of this insurance system suggests that materially it is less helpful than appears at first glance. The inadequacies of unemployment benefits have already been mentioned. Payments made under the other insurance schemes are also very small, and are hedged about with numerous restrictions. But the fundamental inequity of the schemes lies in their financing. Insurance premiums are divided equally between employers and workers (except in the case of accident insurance, whose premiums are paid entirely by employers). The State's contributions are trifling. Inasmuch as the employers probably pass the bulk of their premium payments on to consumers in the form of higher prices, the main burden of insurance is borne in the end by the low-income masses of the population. Furthermore, the funds of the social-insurance agencies have been tapped by the Government as a convenient and important means of stopping holes in its budget and for lending to depressed industries. Only a small part of the receipts have been paid out as benefits to the insured workers. (About three-fourths of the reserves accumulated by the insurance institutions during 1922–35 were used by the Government to finance land reclamation, railways, shipping companies, and other industrial enterprises.) There is also complaint that in rural districts the insurance system works very haphazardly.

There is no doubt, however, that the social-welfare and educational institutions of Fascism provide the working population with numerous benefits. Members of the *Dopolavoro* may at little or no cost travel in the country, receive medical treatment, take part in a variety of sports and pastimes, attend lectures, theaters, and vocational courses. These institutions at the same time are extremely important in serving the political ends of the regime. For one thing, they give employment to many faithful members of the Party. But more significant is their function as media of Fascist propaganda. They are, in fact, one of the major channels through which the Government extends its control over the masses of the people. During his working hours, the laborer has little chance to think about anything but the job before him, and in his leisure time the *Dopolavoro* helps to safeguard him from 'dangerous thoughts.' The benefits of social insurance and *Dopolavoro* are a powerful weapon to keep the workers 'in line.' Indeed, such devices may go far towards winning men to Fascism.

Here, as elsewhere, the Fascists adopted familiar but colorless institutions, infused them with patriotic glamour, presented them as gifts of a fatherly ruler. The payment of old-age pensions becomes an occasion for public celebrations; medals are pinned on zealous workers; prizes are bestowed on long-established peasant families. Thus it may well appear to common men that Fascism understands their language and, as the Duce has said, 'moves towards the people.' In such ways has Fascism found vitality.

The regime makes much of the improvements in public health after 1922, and gives itself the credit for this. Adult and infant mortality rates have declined continually, and the toll of malaria, tuberculosis, typhoid fever, and cholera has been much diminished. But death and morbidity rates had been falling for many years before the advent of Fascism. There is no evidence that the Dictatorship itself has made tremendous contributions in this direction. Much the same must be said of education and literacy. More money is being spent on kindergartens and schools, and the number of persons who can read and write has increased steadily. Yet in many rural communities the schools remain very inadequate. Moreover, it must be kept in mind that under Fascism the schools are a powerful instrument of nationalistic, warlike propaganda. It is not easy for children to resist the attractions of wearing uniforms, playing at soldiers, participating in mass athletics, and taking part in imaginary official duties. Those who turn away from these blandishments are exposed to merciless pressures of social ostracism by their comrades.

Viewed most generously, such welfare services as have developed under Fascism may be a compensation—intangible, but nevertheless significant—for the decline of the workers' wage incomes. But the material living standards of the Italian people have sunk markedly since the advent of the 'labor peace.' This is shown not merely by the movement of wages and employment, but even more definitely by the reduced consumption of many important commodities.

According to official sources, there has been a serious fall in both the quantity and quality of food consumed. A noted Italian statistician stated as early as 1925 that 'the indices of food consumption prove that the Italian people, who, even before the war, were not abundantly nourished from the physiological standpoint, have been compelled to reduce still further their consumption of foods and in the last two years have been in a situation constantly less favorable; yet, in order to adapt themselves to the requirements of new labor conditions, they have had to accept a diet not in accordance with their tastes.' [16] And in 1929 a Fascist deputy in the course of a parliamentary debate declared: 'Our ration is perhaps the lowest in all Europe.' [17] During 1926–35, the amount of wheat available *per capita* fell about ten per cent—that is, to a point apparently lower than in pre-war years. Declines in the *per capita* consumption of other foods during the same period were: meats, 14 per cent; olive oil, 15 per cent; butter and lard, 6 per cent; sugar, 21 per cent; fruits and vegetables, 11 per cent.* A sharp drop in the use of salt implies that less cooked food was being eaten. Consumption of wine—a dietary staple in Italy—also fell considerably. Indeed, despite a measure of economic revival after the Abyssinian War, the consumption of almost every common type of foodstuff in 1936–7 was below the levels of the 1920's.

But, inasmuch as these data are only *national* averages, the food eaten by the poorer workers must have deteriorated cruelly. They may not starve, but their diet is hardly above a subsistence level. In parts of South Italy, it is reported, very many of the peasants during long periods of the year live on a single meal a day of bread and greens. Happily, the leading

---

* In 1934 the people of France consumed *per capita* twice as much meat, three times as much milk, six times as much butter, as the Italians.

Fascist 'labor' newspaper has discovered the merits of a vege-
tarian diet: 'We do not insist that meat must be considered as
one of the major, constant, indispensable articles of popular
diet.' [18] But an Italian dietary expert—apparently not given to
the methods of Coué—has pointed out: 'Malnutrition, by
many held to have gone forever, is returning in wide areas to
the disadvantage of the peasant. . . . Those who are in
places of command would do well to keep their eyes open.' [19]
The man in supreme command is—on the word of one of his
admirers—only too concerned: 'His thoughts are assiduously
occupied with economic problems and he strives to assure
food and work to the laboring classes because the spectacle
of poverty saddens him to the verge of illness.' [20] Yet, in a
speech that Mussolini made in the Chamber of Deputies in
1930, he found advantages in the peculiar habits of his people: 'Fortunately the Italian people is not yet accustomed to
eating several times a day, and, having a modest level of living, feels scarcity and suffering less.' [21]

Consumption of other goods shrank, too. The purchases of
tobacco fell by one-fifth during 1928–35, while clothing and
furniture sales during 1929–34 declined by about a third.
(There appears to have been some recovery in these respects
during 1936–7.) Moreover, the activities of public pawn
shops, municipal lodging houses, and free soup kitchens attest
to the miserable situation of the proletariat.

Housing and sanitary conditions remain deplorable in
many regions. According to an official inquiry, made in 1934,
about one-third of the rural population was then occupying
'almost absolutely uninhabitable' houses. Several hundred
thousand peasants lived with their animals in dark caves and
in hovels made of straw. Another official report showed that
in 1931 nearly half of all urban dwellings were without run-

ning water, one-fourth had no latrines, and more than 95 per cent were innocent of baths. A large proportion of the houses were overcrowded. Of course, these conditions were largely inherited from the past, and cannot be attributed to the Fascist regime. Mussolini himself has agreed that housing is unsatisfactory, especially in smaller towns and villages, and has promised that 'within a few decades all peasants and farm workers must possess large, healthful houses.' [22] Yet, the Fascist Government has done little to improve the situation outside a few districts in cities frequented by tourists. The widely advertised public-works programs have made only insubstantial provision for low-cost housing. Certainly, the construction of workers' houses has not been much accelerated under Fascism, and cannot be compared with contemporary developments in Western European countries. Apparently it has been much more tempting to build showy motor roads, monumental public buildings, and implements of war.

If the workers wonder at a 'proletarian regime' under which their wages buy less and less of the necessities of life, they are reminded of higher values than those of mere food and drink. A Fascist text-book on 'corporative economics' points out that 'the final goal of the general interest, that is, the interest of the State, is always paramount. To this end, the worker must and does direct himself conscientiously. And precisely because the Corporate State considers the worker as the instrument for realizing the superior ends of the Nation, it exalts his function. When Mussolini affirms that the present century is the century of labor, he emphasizes the importance and the power of labor—not merely in the naturalistic sense of the material well-being of many or very many individuals, but also in that ethical sense which is derived from continuous reference to the interests of the Nation.' [23] Such exalted mysticism—or cruel nonsense—is meant to console the people for their poverty!

The corporative machinery for settlement of labor controversies is pointed to as further proof that the 'principle of class-collaboration, of class solidarity, of devotion to the paramount interests of the Nation, has found its realization.' Whenever a dispute between employers and employees arises, an attempt is made to bring about a settlement through mediation by the appropriate syndical representatives of the Ministry of Corporations. If this effort is unsuccessful, resort is had to compulsory arbitration by special 'labor' sessions of the courts. Any other method of settlement, as by direct negotiation between a particular employer and his workers, is prohibited. The 'labor courts'—which have jurisdiction over collective labor disputes—are composed of three ordinary judges and two 'experts in production and labor problems.' * Inasmuch as the 'experts' must be university graduates, there is little likelihood, *a priori*, that the workers' point of view will predominate. Furthermore, the courts have no judicial independence. It is clear, in fact, that their verdicts cannot depart from the policies dictated in superior governmental circles. Yet the labor courts are hailed as the final guarantee of the 'just wage.'

In practice, only a small percentage of disputes have been finally referred to the courts for arbitration. During the years 1927–36, some 954 conflicts over terms of collective contracts were submitted to the Ministry of Corporations for mediation. Most of these were settled through the offices of the Ministry. During the same period, only 14 such disputes were settled by sentence of the labor courts. The tribunals also play a minor role with respect to complaints made by individual workers or employers. Generally, workers suffer contractual

* Ordinary local courts judge individual labor disputes.

violations to take place without protest, and complain only when they are dismissed. Most of the individual controversies are settled by the syndical officials, and usually their decisions favor the complainants. But punishment of employers who violate contracts appears to be rare. Moreover, the whole machinery of mediation and arbitration moves at a painfully slow and tortuous pace.

The Duce once informed the president of the Confederation of Industrialists: 'I assure Signor Benni that so long as I am in power the employers have nothing to fear from the labor courts.' [24] Certainly, the decisions of the courts show no undue sympathy for the workers. Not once have they required an increase in wages. A number of the collective disputes run along a curiously uniform pattern: first the employers demand a substantial cut in wages; the workers-syndicate officials refuse this demand, but offer to accept a smaller reduction; finally, the labor courts fix the actual wage cut at or near the level suggested by the workers' representatives. Thus wages are slashed, but it is possible to claim a 'victory' for labor. In the proceedings before the judges the 'representatives' show an extraordinary spirit of self-sacrifice and accommodation to the interests of employers. Their characteristic words of consolation to the workers who see their wages fall are: 'Keep your spirits up!' Mussolini's Government has then to be hailed in telegrams from the grateful laborers as 'the true protector of the working people.' The demagogues never weary of repeating that 'Fascism's exaltation of labor has been always directed to making workers the predominant political and economic element of the community. . . . The whole Fascist morality is a morality of labor.'

Another important aspect of Fascist labor policy is the attempt to 'deproletarianize' the rural laborers. According to a prominent Fascist official, Italy must have, not casual farm wage workers, but 'genuine peasants, attached to the soil, loving the soil, who do not ask the impossible, who know how to content themselves.' [25] To this end, the agricultural workers must be 'bound to the soil' by receiving a greater proportion of their wages in farm products rather than money, by changing day-laborers into share-croppers, and by encouraging share-tenancy contracts. Thus, it is said, Fascism seeks to change 'the proletarian, who is not and cannot be a Nationalist, and even less a Fascist, into a type of artisan who can be made to feel the nature of property.' [26]

Progress certainly has been made in the efforts to pay farm-hands' wages in kind and to extend share-cropping. This undoubtedly is advantageous to employers who are hard-pressed financially. Payment of wages in produce permits them to cut down their working-cash balances, and gives them an opportunity to shift on to their employees a part of their business risks. But its advantage to the 'transformed' worker is less evident, although a Fascist newspaper has pointed out that he 'will thus acquire a keener sense of responsibility and will gain a closer understanding of the process of production.' The cropper cultivates under the close direction of the employer, has no independence in choice of crops or methods of work, and is subject to the employer's discipline. As before, he is a dependent laborer, paid in kind instead of in cash, with few or no guarantees of income and working hours, and is more firmly bound to the landlord than the wage-paid hand. A hint at the dangers involved in this practice was given in a syndicate meeting: 'In not a few cases share-cropping degenerates and comes to represent in the hands of less correct proprietors a means of imposing on the croppers heavy uncompensated burdens. . . . Who wonders then if so many peasants and workers want payment in cash, considering it as a delivery from servitude?' [27] But the Ministry of Corporations has described share-cropping contracts as 'a safeguard against the risks of sudden convulsion and upheaval.' [28] And this perhaps is the ultimate advantage that the rulers of Italy saw in their goal of 'binding' the worker to the soil.

Here, indeed, is the essence of Fascist labor organization. It is a mechanism for binding the workers firmly to the employing groups, and, beyond, to the political chiefs of the State. It is the ball and chain that reduces wage-earners to helplessness, making them into passive raw materials for the 'higher' purposes of the Nation. Whatever strength the workers once had to resist the downward pressures of employers on wages and to influence governmental policies has disappeared with the destruction of the old economic and political labor movement. Is it mere chance that the establishment of the Fascist labor controls coincided with the beginning of a period of rapidly falling wages? Fascist apologists insist that the stabilization of the lira in 1927 and the world depression after 1929 were responsible for severe price deflation and shrinkage of markets in Italy. Business activity of necessity fell off, and therefore the 'possibilities of production' were reduced. But this is an admission that Fascism has been unable to provide a solution for the crises of capitalism. Rather, it perpetuates an inherently unstable set of economic institutions. It remains that the Fascist regime has given the workers a 'higher social justice' curiously compounded of glowing praise, material impoverishment, and shattered hopes for freedom. 'With regard to labor,' a Blackshirt hierarch has observed, 'Fascism is superbly revolutionary . . . Fascism has always exalted labor, in all its forms, as the highest and noblest aspect of life.' [29]

# V : BREAD AND LAND

In the villages, as well as in the cities, Fascism preaches its doctrine of class-collaboration. A country whose life is fundamentally agricultural makes it expedient for Mussolini and his followers to pose as champions of the peasant. They assert that Fascism is concerned unceasingly with the welfare of the rural population. Mussolini tells the villagers: 'I am proud to be your friend, your brother, your leader. . . . Only with Fascism have the peasants come into their full rights. . . . The people who abandon the land are condemned to decadence. . . . As between the city and the village, I am for the village. . . . I have willed that agriculture take first place in the Italian economy. . . . Italy must be ruralized, even if billions and a half century are required.' [1] In the harvest season the Duce is in the habit of going to a wheat-field near Rome. There, stripped to his waist, he is photographed hard at work amidst a crowd of threshers. He has also won some fame for a poem in honor of bread.

The Fascists sing the praises of the simple rural life. A predominantly agricultural society with its high birth-rate, they assert, not only assures a constant growth of the population, but it also guarantees the moral and physical health of the race, safeguards the high ideals of life, expresses the beauty of creative labor. 'In the cities,' the orators say, 'where all try to live the comfortable life, where the most bitter selfishness finds expression, where the sense of human solidarity has been hardest hit, not only in appearance but in actual fact, these qualities are fast disappearing.' [2] Perhaps it is only their loyalty to official duty that has made the politicos remain in the poisonous atmosphere of the cities.

Italy under Fascism, therefore, must go back to the land. To combat the drift to the cities, the peasants are to be bound firmly to the soil. The casual, shifting farm workers will be given a stake in the land by being converted into share-croppers and tenants; the tenants and small proprietors, in turn, will be safeguarded and increased in numbers. The *latifondi* of the South may eventually, under pressure of competition from the favored intensive farmers, be split up voluntarily by their owners. However, all property rights—the pillars of social order—must be preserved; therefore proposals for general expropriation of the large landowners are rejected. Only the failure of a proprietor to fulfill his 'social duty' can justify the seizure of his land by the State. Furthermore, large areas of land reclaimed from swamps and dunes are to be colonized by peasant farmers. This will provide room at home for the land-hungry masses and also increase the nation's ability to produce foodstuffs. Agricultural output is to be vigorously encouraged, with special emphasis on intensive cultivation. Above all, the nation is to be made self-sufficient in its primary food, wheat.

Wheat is grown everywhere in Italy, in all regions and on every type of farm. But industrialization and a rapidly growing population after 1900 expanded wheat requirements far beyond the domestic output. Italy, already importing most of its basic industrial raw materials, also had to buy more and more of its breadstuffs abroad. The World War plainly revealed her serious dependence on overseas countries for coal, cotton, oil, and wheat. Thus, any power that commanded the entrances to the Mediterranean might control the destiny of Italy. For many Italians this situation was a cause for patriotic concern. The conviction spread that strenuous efforts must be made to win a greater degree of self-sufficiency. But wheat was the only major import commodity that could be produced in larger quantities at home.

This was the motive expressed by the Fascist Government when, in the middle of 1925, it launched its famous 'Battle of Wheat.' A desire for political prestige may well have played a part, too. The Matteotti crisis, only recently overcome, had severely shaken confidence in the regime. An aggressive and well-publicized campaign to raise more wheat must make a strong appeal to all nationally-minded Italians, and so might help to build up faith in the Government.

The goal of the Battle was to 'free Italy from the slavery of foreign bread' in the shortest possible time. It was hoped that this goal might be reached within four or five years. Because the rational limit of wheat acreage had already been overstepped, it was recognized that little could be expected from more extensive cultivation of the cereal. However, in view of the inefficiency of much wheat farming in Italy, victory seemed to lie in the direction of intensified efforts on existing acreage.

Various subsidies were adopted by the Government to encourage a greater use of fertilizers and farm machinery. The prices of fuel used in tractors and of chemical fertilizers were reduced. The Government promoted the building of silos, the distribution of selected wheat seeds, and the use of seed-sorting machines and motor-ploughs. It fostered drainage projects and the construction of roads, stalls, troughs, and the like, on uncultivated land adaptable to wheat. Technical aid and research were also encouraged. At the same time, propaganda weapons—through the medium of newspapers, schools, churches, radios, motor caravans—were wielded to whip up a 'wheat consciousness' among all the people.

But the essence of the Battle was the levying of very heavy duties on wheat imports. In order to stimulate production (and incidentally to check consumption) it was necessary to maintain domestic wheat prices at levels profitable to the high-cost Italian farmers—that is, at levels far above world market prices. Beginning in 1925 the tariff was successively raised until it became practically prohibitive to wheat imports.* High tariffs were also placed on wheat flour, corn, and other competitive cereals. These measures, together with a system of compulsory, pooled sales of farmers' market supplies, flour-mixing regulations, and the control of enterprise exerted by the official corporative agencies, enabled the Government to fix wheat prices that were highly favorable to Italian producers. The gap between domestic and foreign prices broadened markedly, and the purchasing power of wheat in the home market rose. After 1925, Italian farmers found that their wheat on the average could buy more than a third again as much as before the beginning of the Battle.

Given such a powerful pecuniary encouragement, it is not surprising that Italy has eventually come close to self-sufficiency in breadstuffs. Largely because of more intensive and more rational cultivation, the national output after 1930 rose to levels forty to sixty per cent higher than before the World War. In consequence, imports were drastically reduced. Only in seasons of unfavorable weather was it necessary to draw on foreign supplies in substantial quantities. The Government, characteristically, hailed good crops as the result of its policies and blamed Providence for the poor crops.

Thus the Fascist regime could claim that the Battle of Wheat was crowned with victory. It made the most of cele-

---

* A poor crop in 1936 forced a reduction in the duty so as to admit more foreign wheat. But quota controls have been retained over such imports.

brating yet another triumph. But victory was purchased at the cost of seriously unbalancing Italian agriculture and of imposing heavy burdens on consumers.

Continual emphasis on more and yet more wheat production; the slight attention given by the Government's technical advisors to crop-rotation, animal husbandry, and general farm management; the highly favorable domestic wheat prices—all drew interest away from other important branches of agriculture. Tree crops and livestock suffered most from the onesided wheat policy.

Italy is naturally well suited for the production of fruits, vegetables, nuts, and vines. The mild climate and the soil are favorable to most temperate fruits and vegetables, and also to many subtropical plants. Because of the extension of the country from north to south, it is possible to spread vegetable production over most of the year. Thus, Italy has special advantage in supplying southern fruits, wines, and early vegetables to European markets. But she failed to exploit this advantage in the face of growing world trade during the 1920's. Other countries—notably Spain, Italy's closest competitor in this field—forged ahead.

More serious was the decline of the livestock industry. Experts had long urged that this industry—backward both in extent and methods—be expanded in order to strengthen the country's agriculture. But after the beginning of the wheat campaign there was a general decline of the farm-animal population. In South Italy the reduction in all groups of animals was astonishingly drastic. Most conspicuous was a huge disappearance of goats, the 'cows of the poor.'

The explanation for these unfavorable developments is not far to seek. Attention was concentrated on raising the technical level of wheat production, to the neglect of fruits and

vegetables. Moreover, the high duties on cereals upset old relationships between various branches of agriculture. Italian
livestock producers, operating with high-cost grains and fod-
ders, could not resist the increased competition of cheap foreign meats. The wheat program, too, made profitable a shifting of pasture land into grain fields. Heavy taxes on goats and
on meat consumption were also depressing factors. Imports
of live animals, butter, and wool rose markedly after 1925.
Eggs, formerly a significant export, had to be imported. Italy's
dependence on foreign supplies of animal products was increased. Thus, with respect to her international trade balance,
it is not enough to point only to the reduction in wheat
imports. Account must also be taken of the greater imports
and smaller exports of many other agricultural commodities,
for which the wheat policy was in large degree responsible.

It is South Italy, always the stepchild, that has borne the
main burden of the extreme emphasis on wheat and the neglect of other agricultural industries. There, the physical conditions are hostile to efficient grain production. Wheat-farm-
ing actually tends to reduce the productivity of the soil.
Nevertheless, nearly half of Italy's total wheat area is in the
South. This extensive cultivation can be explained largely by
the insistent desire of the many small peasant farmers to produce enough breadstuffs for their own needs, regardless of
disadvantages of soil, climate, or land-elevation. On the other
hand, the South is adapted to certain types of production,
such as citrus fruits, vines, figs, olives, almonds, grasses, and
forage plants. Furthermore, the manure of pasture animals
and soil-building clovers and beans would enrich the soil and
make it ultimately more productive even in cereals. The old
problem of inefficient production in South Italy would prob-

ably find a partial solution in the encouragement of fruit and vegetable cultivation and of animal husbandry. But the Battle of Wheat, by leading to an increase of wheat acreage and a decline of livestock, made even more pronounced the frequently deplored one-sidedness of Southern agriculture.

Thus, as a result of the Battle of Wheat important branches of agriculture retrogressed. And this outweighed the undoubted advances in farming techniques to which the Battle contributed. Obviously, whatever the avowed objectives of the campaign, in practice it certainly did not help to rationalize Italian agriculture.

Insofar as the wheat tariff and the resultant high wheat prices are of financial help to agriculture, such help has gone mainly to the landlords and wealthier farmers. Only they, after all, are able to sell substantial amounts of wheat, and therefore can profit from the price-supporting measures. On the other hand, share-tenants and small-holders consume the bulk of their own output, and at times even must buy flour, bread, and pastes to meet all their needs.* And most rural wage-workers have primarily a consumers' interest in wheat. For them, the tariff is only something that raises the cost of their bread. The Battle, then, has tended to sharpen the inequitable distribution of agricultural income. The majority of the rural population have actually been harmed by the wheat tariff, as well as by industrial tariffs.

As for the wage-earners of towns and cities, their contribution towards the 'Wheat Victory' has been higher living costs and reduced consumption. In terms of wage incomes, breadstuffs became decidedly more expensive after the initiation of the Battle. The average industrial hourly wage in 1933–6

* It is estimated that two-fifths of the Italian cereal production is directly consumed by the peasants.

could buy only three-quarters as much bread as before 1925. (Bread and pastes, it must be remembered, bulk large in the diet of most Italians.) During the ten years after 1925, Italian consumers paid a premium of roughly 32,000 million lire on their wheat—a gigantic hidden subsidy going mainly to the large and medium-sized landowners. Had there been no tariff, all the wheat consumed during this period could have been bought for one-third less than it actually cost.

High prices led to a substantial decline of wheat consumption. The average quantity available *per capita* fell 15 per cent during 1925–35. That is, the larger home production was not enough to make up for the curtailed imports. The price-supporting measures of the Fascist wheat campaign made for 'self-sufficiency,' not only by raising production, but also by forcing consumers to tighten their belts.

The Fascists insist that to become a world power Italy must win independence in her food supplies, even if it means even greater immediate poverty for the masses and possible loss of foreign markets for Italian goods. Yet from the standpoint of military necessity, the Battle has been of doubtful value. Certain Italian economists have argued that a 'battle *against* wheat' and encouragement of livestock production would be more helpful in raising Italy's ability to feed herself in a period of emergency. Moreover, Italy needs not only wheat, but also fats, petroleum, coal, iron, cotton, wool, and other materials that must come to a large extent from beyond the Mediterranean. A genuine blockade of the approaches to that sea must quickly embarrass even a Fascist Italy that has freed herself from 'enslavement to foreign bread.'

The Battle of Wheat has catered to no interests save those of propertied groups and of the prestige-hungry Fascist regime. The well-being of the millions of small peasant farmers and of the agricultural and industrial workers would be served far better by cheap manufactured goods and cheap food, which would call for abolition of high import duties on industrial products and on wheat.

More spectacular even than the Battle of Wheat has been the Fascist program of land reclamation. According to the Duce, reclamation would 'give land and bread to millions of Italians in the future.' [3]

For generations the Italian farmers and peasants have fought against wind and water for possession of the soil. Throughout large parts of Italy the deforested hills and mountains are constantly being eroded and silt-laden rivers threaten to pile up water-damming barriers in the plains. This has made vast regions of rocky, sterile highlands and marshy wastes. But for centuries old fields were saved and new lands won by the continual, patient building of dykes, terraces, drainage and irrigation ditches. Indeed, many of the areas most fertile today were reclaimed long before Italy's unification. But the earlier reclamation works for the most part were of small scope and limited effect. Although land-owners joined together to clear and irrigate land, their limited resources prevented them from going far. Even before 1860, State aid was being extended to private drainage schemes. After unification the national Government took part in reclamation on a steadily bigger scale. As the years passed, a tendency towards greater State initiative and authority and towards larger-scale works became more and more pronounced. Actual achievements before 1922—always minimized by the Fascist regime, which sought to give the impression that it had virtually invented reclamation—were very substantial.

Viewed in broad perspective, Fascist reclamation policy is

a continuance of pre-war development towards a broader comprehension of the problem and towards increasing governmental activity. Under Fascism, as in earlier times, too, the Government's concern for reclamation has been markedly influenced by the financial situation of landowners, the degree of unemployment, and the condition of the State's finances.

For four or five years after the March on Rome the Fascist Government showed less active interest in reclamation than did its immediate predecessors, for it was engrossed in budgetary economies and in promoting industrial revival. Moreover, unemployment was not serious. But with the onset of agricultural depression, the Government began to display a keen concern in large-scale reclamation. Mussolini now declared: 'It is our task to change beyond recognition the physical and spiritual face of our country within the space of ten years.' [4] During 1927 an immense, 'integrated' program, that would eventually give new land to millions of peasants, was announced. A law of December 1928, proclaimed amidst tremendous hubbub, called for an expenditure of 7,000 million lire for land reclamation over a period of fourteen years, 4,350 millions to be supplied by the Government and 2,650 millions by the landowners. The more important projects were to be carried out largely at public expense, with compulsory contributions by the owners. Minor works might be executed by the farmers with the help of governmental subsidies. 'Reclamation' was to include not only drainage, reforestation, and irrigation, but also provision of roads, drinking water, farm buildings, and electricity. Larger income expected from improved lands was to be remuneration for the landowners' expenditures. The territory to be reclaimed was divided into districts, and the owners in each district were called upon to form an association that would plan and direct the work under the general supervison of the Government. Such an association might be formed either voluntarily by the individuals owning a major portion of the land in a particular district, or under compulsion. In any case, its decisions bound all landowners of the district. If a proprietor was unable or unwilling to shoulder his share of the expenses, he might be expropriated (with compensation, of course). The associations appeared to be dominated by the bigger landlords.

According to the Government, the total cost of the works undertaken during 1928–36 was 6,400 million gold lire, compared with 3,300 million during 1870–1928. By 1936, reclamation projects had been 'completed' or were 'under way' on one-sixth of the country's total area. But this claim is very misleading. For one thing, nearly half of the 'reclamation area' was land long since under intensive cultivation. There, 'reclamation' simply consisted of keeping drainage and irrigation ditches, dykes, and the like, in repair. Under the Fascist program, too, the meaning of 'land reclamation' was stretched to include almost any kind of work, from drainage to road-building and provision of electricity, that might permit more intensive farming. Furthermore, operations had scarcely been started on another large portion of the area. Also, in their enthusiasm, the publicists were not above claiming projects undertaken years before 1922 as purely Fascist achievements.

Nevertheless, even after deflating the preposterous claims of the advertising agents, the Fascist *bonifica integrale* ('integral reclamation') has been impressive. Considerable advances have been made in drainage and other improvements of lands in the lower Po valley, in Tuscany, and in the vicinities of Rome and Naples. Accomplishments have been more modest in the heel and toe of the Peninsula and in Sicily.

Unfortunately for reclamation elsewhere, there has been an extraordinary concentration of work in one relatively small area, the famous 'Pontine Marshes.' This region of about 185,000 acres of marsh and dunes—within 40 miles of Rome—provided the Fascist Government with an opportunity to carry out a project of enormous publicity value. The *Agro Pontino*—for centuries malaria-ridden, hardly populated, and little cultivated—had in the past been the object of several unsuccessful attempts at drainage. Its conversion (regardless of cost) into a 'new and Fascist province' of small farms cultivated by war-veteran colonists must become an important advertisement for the regime.

The tasks of reclaiming and colonizing the *Pontino* were turned over to the *Opera Nazionale Combattenti* (the war-veterans' association), the governmental propagandists glorified the venture, and public funds were poured into it lavishly. These huge expenditures—amounting after 1932 to nearly a third of all outlays for reclamation and reforestation throughout the country—imposed a heavy burden on the general reclamation program. Other projects, many of which would have had greater social and economic (although less political) value, suffered. Moreover, some of the land in the *Pontino* has proved to be poor and incapable of supporting the many colonists intended for it. (According to the authorities, 50,000 peasants are eventually to be settled there. At the end of 1935 the number of colonist families established in the *Pontino* was 2,215, comprising about 19,000 persons.) There is danger, too, that large expenditures will have to be continued for a long time to prevent the drained areas from turning into arid dunes. Nevertheless, the scheme has been highly successful as a sample of 'what Fascism can do.' Together with the punctuality of Fascist railway trains, the drainage of the 'Pontine marshes' is rated by Mussolini's foreign admirers as among the very greatest of his achievements.

Only a small fraction of the huge financial burdens entailed by the Fascist reclamation program has fallen immediately on the Government and landowners. The Government's share is to be paid largely in instalments over a period of 30 years. The obligations of the owners also take the form of annual payments, covering both the capital value of their burden and the interest thereon. Most of the funds immediately needed were supplied by credit institutions, especially the savings banks and insurance companies. It seems unlikely, however, that even the large sums envisaged will be enough to complete satisfactorily all the works undertaken. The pressure to provide jobs for the growing number of unemployed, and to satisfy the insistent demands for politically spectacular achievements, has evidently forced the reclamation officials to venture beyond reasonable limits in authorizing new works. As a result, some technically ill-advised work has been initiated, farm indebtedness has grown enormously, and the influence of financial institutions over agriculture has been extended. The severe decline of agricultural commodity prices after 1927 has aggravated the problems of landed debt. The original plans for financing reclamation have had to be modified considerably, and the Government has been obliged to rescue many mortgage-ridden landlords. With the initiation of the 'imperial' phase of Fascism (in 1935) the outlays for land reclamation were drastically cut. An effort was made to abandon all works not urgently needed. In 1937 a high Fascist official admitted that 'reclamation is marking time for reasons of a contingent nature. But it is hoped that the work can be got under way again.' [5]

Fascist enthusiasts have extolled the reclamation program

as primarily a boon to the landless peasants. By giving them new land at home, they say, Italy will have a substitute for emigration. Furthermore, it is claimed that the *latifondi*, in consequence of sales required by reclamation financing, will finally be parcelled among the peasantry. For the benefit of the masses, much publicity has been given to the proposed expropriation of landowners who have failed to fulfill their 'social duty' of improving their land. This is also pointed to as a method of breaking up the great estates.

Here too the gap between Fascist theory and practice is very wide. Actually, the land reclamation schemes have offered little land to the rural masses. Although a large part of the costs have been defrayed out of public revenues, the peasants have been given no preferential rights in the reclaimed lands. * And the suggestion that the big estates would be reduced through forced sales or expropriations has not been realized. Little land has been sold by the great proprietors for the purpose of raising reclamation funds. There was no need for them to be worried by the politicians' talk of 'social duties' and confiscation. By the end of 1935 only 67,000 acres—less than a tenth of one per cent of all farm land—had been expropriated because of the landowners' inability to meet their reclamation obligations.

The *bonifica integrale* has not even led to appreciable settlement of landless farm laborers on the soil as share-tenants or share-croppers. In 1930–36 some 8,857 families (that is, not one per cent of all rural wage-workers' families) were thus established in Italy. Moreover, the land-improvement programs have had unfortunate consequences for the mountain peasantry, which depends for much of its living

---

* With the limited exception of the war-veterans favored by the National War-Veteran's Association.

on animal husbandry. Pasture lands have been taken from many shepherds by reforestation schemes, and some reclamation works in the plains have also had this effect. The Fascist wheat and taxation policies, too, by tending to depress the sheep and goat population, have brought distress to the highland communities. It is not surprising, then, that a marked depopulation of the mountain regions is taking place. These are aspects of the reverse side of Fascist reclamation, aspects that the Government is careful not to reveal. To be sure, the *bonifica* did help relieve unemployment: about a third of all laborers engaged in public works in 1931–5 were busy on reclamation schemes. (But this was at most only six per cent of the total number of jobless.) And it has also made contributions to the public health, especially in reducing the breeding places of malarial mosquitoes.

Such criticisms are no denial of the urgent need of land improvement, irrigation, and reforestation in order to raise Italy's agricultural productivity. Indeed, the country could well do with vastly greater expenditures for such purposes. Much more might already have been accomplished if public funds had gone less into military paraphernalia and more into reclamation. But the character of Fascist reclamation policy is such that it can contribute little towards improving the living levels of the Italian peasantry. For the Fascist undertakings are too greatly subordinated to political motives and to the interests of certain big landlords.

Despite the politicians' boasts of giving the peasants a greater stake in the soil, most Italian farm land continues to be owned by relatively few proprietors. The Fascist era has seen an extension of share-cropping, certainly. But it also is marked by increased difficulties for small proprietors, especially in the South, and even greater subordination of the peasants to the interests of absentee ownership. On being asked privately why Fascism has not brought about agrarian reform, the Minister of Agriculture replied: 'We cannot confiscate the property of the landlords; we are Fascists, not Socialists.' [6]

It is true that the Italian census data show a decline, from 1921 to 1936, of slightly more than two millions in the number of farm wage-workers. Government spokesmen frequently point to this as evidence that the policy of 'deproletarization' is having effect. But they do not add that the number of 'operating owners' also fell nearly three-quarters of a million in the same period. Other data point to an increase in peasant proprietorship during 1915–26. Therefore it is reasonable to infer that a serious elimination of independent farmers took place after 1926—that is, in the very years when the regime was supposedly strengthening the small peasants! On the other hand, the number of cash-and share-tenants and share-croppers rose by about 1,200,000 during 1921–36. Apparently, many tenants who had become landowners during and immediately after the World War were forced by financial difficulties in later years to return to their old status.

While farm-tenancy has become more prominent, the economic position of tenants has deteriorated. Terms of share-tenancy contracts made after 1922 were decidedly less favorable to the peasants than those concluded immediately after the war. A 'Charter of Share-Tenancy,' embodying basic rules for share-farming agreements, was announced in 1933. The Charter was a victory for the landlords, depriving tenants of concessions that they had won in earlier years. It specifies, for example, that tenancy contracts may have a duration of only one year, that they may be abrogated on six months' notice, that the administration of the farm is to be absolutely in the hands of the owner, that the tenant is responsible for all the farm work (even if outside labor must be hired), that all members of the tenant's household are subject to the terms of the contract.

The Government's policy of enclosing common lands, too, was not calculated to aid the peasants. For centuries the inhabitants of many villages had possessed rights of pasturing and watering their stock, cutting wood, and even tilling and living on certain nominally private lands. These lands helped provide the income of thousands of small peasants. But they were irksome to the nominal proprietors, inasmuch as they tended to limit their authority and income, and complicated the transfer of titles. Under a law of May 1924, steps were taken to abolish these common rights. Thus these peasants, themselves owning little or no land, were deprived of pasturage and firewood, and the small cash payment that they received was but a poor compensation for their loss.

'Our regime,' a Fascist authority has observed, 'believes in the fundamental importance of landed private property. . . . It scrupulously respects the principle of proprietorship.'[7] According to the agricultural census of 1930 (the most recent), 36 per cent of the 4.2 million farm enterprises in Italy were less than 2.5 acres in size, and 55 per cent covered only 2.5 to 25 acres. Yet these two classes of farms together comprised only a third of all the agricultural land. That is, the remaining two-thirds of the land was included in less than ten per cent of the *farms*. Other official data showed that two-thirds of the land belonged to only 3.4 per cent of all *landowners*. It is said that almost half of all the land belongs to less that a half of one per cent of the agricultural population! Thus the peasants still are separated from control of the land they till, and with less hope than before of rising in the economic scale.

Fascism, then, despite its pretensions to an 'eminently rural policy,' has done little or nothing towards solution of the basic problem of Italy's rural masses: the problem of backward techniques, low production, and resultant poverty. Above all, their welfare demands a removal of tariff barriers erected in the interests of industrial and landed property, an end to the enormous wastes of military display and imperial adventure, a complete reorganization of land tenure and taxation, and opportunity for emigration.

## VI : PROPERTY AND PROFITS

FASCISM bears the two faces of the ancient Roman deity Janus. To conservatively-minded men, it appears to be a guardian of the old values; but to many of the heterodox it represents the promise of a new and better society.

From the first, the leaders of Fascism were at pains to make clear—to the capitalists and landlords—that they had no intention of destroying the traditional basis of Italian economic life. Thus, early in 1923, Mussolini generously promised that 'the Government will accord full freedom to private enterprise and will abandon all intervention in private economy.' [1] Eleven years later he repeated: 'Corporative economy respects the principle of private property. Private property completes human personality.' [2] But other audiences were told that Fascism was establishing a new social order, fundamentally different from Capitalism as well as Socialism, which would regenerate 'proletarian' Italy and enshrine the virtues of labor. In 1934 Mussolini described the corporative economy as 'no longer an economic system that puts the accent on individual profits, but [one that is] concerned with the collective interest. . . . If the past century was the century of the power of capital, so the twentieth century is that of the power and the glory of labor.' [3]

The Charter of Labor remains on comfortable middle ground. It explains that 'the Corporate State considers private enterprise in the sphere of production to be the most effective and useful instrument in the interest of the Nation.' This has been soothing to the traditionalists. However, the

Charter adds that 'State intervention in economic production arises only when private initiative is lacking or insufficient, or when the political interests of the State are involved.' In the minds of 'left-wing' Fascists, this has aroused visions of a new collective economy. Now and then, too, it has injected vague fears into the minds of the propertied. Yet these declarations of the Charter amount to no more than a statement of the customary relations between State and private enterprise throughout the capitalist world.

Fascism rose to power as a preventive reaction, defending the pecuniary and sentimental interests of the propertied and quasi-propertied groups of towns and country from the specter of revolution. And certainly during the first years of the Fascist era, the new regime valiantly served these interests— in deeds if not altogether in words—at the expense of the underlying population. It not only sought to safeguard existing property rights, but also fostered further industrialization and concentration of business enterprise. Moreover, the regime promised to rehabilitate the country economically, as well as politically. In 1924 Mussolini said, 'If we are left in power for five or ten years, Italy will be rich, satisfied and prosperous.' [4] Yet Fascism could not solve the basic difficulties of Italian capitalism. The deepening economic crisis in latter years forced business enterprise to rest more and more on the support of the State. As the economic role of the State grew, a subtle shift of spirit and purposes took place. Governmental support of the going economic order called for an increasing army of intruding officials, for a bureaucratic formalization of business affairs. And the bureaucracy developed ends of its own, associated with holding and enlarging its security and power—ends that diverged from those of the traditional propertied interests. Thus, despite all formal pronouncements, perhaps even unconsciously, Fascism seemed to be evolving into a tyranny over all but a very few of the Italian people.

The first years after the March on Rome—that is, the period 1922–26—saw a rapid expansion of industrial and commercial activity. Fascist writers accounted for this by pointing to the 'social order' established under their regime. This meant, no doubt, that business men had been freed from the restraints imposed by the old labor unions. It was a period that might aptly be termed 'the dictatorship of big business.' Mild currency inflation and cheap money, a tax policy favorable to property accumulation, international economic recovery, the protection of a high tariff wall, imports of foreign capital, * were other important encouragements to the business traffic. In this happy atmosphere, Italian industry rapidly expanded. Production increased more than 50 per cent during 1922–5. The durable-goods industries, especially, made marked advances over their former levels. By 1926, steel and iron production was nearly double that of 1913; motor-car manufacturing had risen to one-eighth of total European production, and over half of the output was exported; the shipbuilding industry met domestic requirements and began to compete in foreign markets; hydro-electric power production was four times greater than before the war. Italy had become the principal European producer and the world's leading exporter of rayon. The machinery, electrical, rubber, and chemical industries also grew impressively.

Italy's foreign trade boomed. The value of merchandise imports and exports in 1926 was about 90 per cent greater

---

* A loan of $100,000,000 was obtained by the Government from American financiers in December 1925. About 4,000 million lire were invested by foreigners in Italian securities during 1926–8.

than in 1922. Capital investments in industry increased appreciably. New investments (net) in stock companies amounted to 2,000 million lire in 1923, 5,000 millions in 1924, and 8,000 millions in 1925. The stock markets were very active, commodity prices rose, unemployment was negligible. Net profits declared by business companies rose from 1.7 per cent of their total capital in 1922 to over 8 per cent in 1925 and 7 per cent in 1926.

But business expansion was based on unsteady speculative foundations. Domestic purchasing power did not rise sufficiently to warrant the growing productive capacity of industry. And the possibilities of export trade were overestimated. Costs were still comparatively high, for Italian industry was not technically on a par with that in other countries. Excess plant capacity was most marked in the rayon, shipbuilding, chemical, and sugar industries.

At this moment the Government undertook to end the inflationary movement by stabilizing the lira. The motives behind Mussolini's dramatic words in August 1926—'I will fight for the lira with my last breath and to my last drop of blood'—were never made clear. During the months that followed this declaration, measures were taken by the Government to deflate the currency, reduce money circulation, and build up reserves of the banks of issue. At the end of 1927 the lira was stabilized at the rate of 19 to the dollar. This was a pronounced overvaluation in terms of foreign currencies. In justification, it was said that economic development during 1923–6 had been 'artificial,' that an end had to be put to the burdens imposed by inflation on persons with fixed incomes, that industrial expansion had to be curbed and turned into saner channels. It was suggested that the lira was stabilized at a high level in order to safeguard the numerous middle-class *rentiers*, who were a significant element in the mass basis of the regime. But perhaps national prestige—a desire to make the lira more valuable than the French franc, only recently stabilized—was the most important consideration. Certainly, the stabilization ran counter to the wishes of bankers and big business men. No longer were they sole masters of the house.

At any rate, these deflationary measures abruptly halted the industrial boom and precipitated a severe recession. Stabilization brought an end to the easy profits that had come to speculators. Domestic prices began to fall, and business activity contracted. Internal debtors found their real burdens greatly increased by the declining price level. Many small and insecurely financed firms were forced to the wall. Costs of production in Italy were thrown out of line with world prices. The export trades were badly hit: by the end of 1928 the lira volume of exports had fallen more than 20 per cent below the level of 1926.

In order to readjust domestic prices, pressure was exerted by the Government to force down wages, living costs, and interest rates. The impotence of the workers made drastic wage cuts relatively easy to impose.

After 1929 the depression assumed far more serious proportions. In Mussolini's words: 'Just as we were almost in sight of land, the American crisis of 24 October 1929 drove us back into the high seas.' Italy was engulfed in the world crisis. * The Government's insistence on holding the lira to the 1927 level, in the face of falling world-market prices, called for further deflationary measures, especially in the form of wage cuts. Industrial production contracted still more. In

---

* It is possible, however, that the deflationary policy begun in 1927 may have softened the impact on Italy of the world-market collapse.

1932 it was at least 25 per cent less than in 1928, and it continued at low levels during 1933–4. A third of productive capacity in 1934 was said to be unused. Foreign trade fell off even more conspicuously. By 1934, in value terms it was less than a third of what it had been in 1926. Even allowing for the intervening fall in prices, this was an enormous decline. Revenues from shipping services, tourist trade, and emigrant remittances, dropped 60 per cent during 1929–32. The writing-down of corporation capital in 1931–2 totalled 16,000 million lire. Net declared profits of stock companies fell from 6 per cent of total capital in 1928 to 0.6 per cent in 1931. In 1932 there were net losses of one per cent. The number of business failures rose from 7,600 in 1926 to an annual average of 12,000 in 1929–33. Protests of commercial bills also became very numerous. The army of totally unemployed workers increased to more than a million in 1934. National income was reduced by perhaps one-third from 1928 to 1931.

The most important long-run consequences of the severe crisis that overwhelmed the Italian economy after 1927 was a sweeping movement of big business combination and growing dependence of banking and heavy industries on State support. Increasingly, the Government intervened in order to prevent widespread business collapse. In latter years, the growing concern with colonial war and preparation for war elsewhere accelerated the tendency towards bureaucratization of the economy. The interpenetration of government and big business became well-nigh inextricable.

The pressures of the business recession stimulated efforts to cut production costs and to control or eliminate competition in important branches of industry. Output and marketing programs were co-ordinated. It was, too, a period of industrial rationalization and standardization of productive and distributive methods. Weak firms were eliminated through the processes of merger and bankruptcy. The rationalization movement was sponsored by the Confederation of Industry and by the Government.

More conspicuous was a rapid concentration of business enterprise. The collapse of prices, production, and profits put many firms in extreme difficulties. To escape the rigors of intensive competition, agreements were made for price-fixing, production control, sharing of markets, establishment of sales syndicates. The concentration movement also took the form of outright consolidation of concerns in holding companies and in mergers and amalgamations. The Fascist Government actively encouraged these developments. As early as June 1927 it facilitated stock-company mergers by granting tax concessions. It also supported the formation of industrial ententes and agreements, and even participated in the formation of several cartels. * In 1933 a law was enacted requiring the consent of the Ministry of Corporations before new industrial plants could be opened or existing ones expanded. Thus the Government was in a position to forbid the erection of factories that might threaten the profits of going concerns.

During the ten years before July 1927 only 160 business mergers and amalgamations had taken place. But from mid-1927 to the end of 1929, 221 mergers—involving a capitalization of 10,000 million lire and eliminating 878 firms—were recorded. In 1930–32 an additional 364 firms disappeared in

---

* A law of 1932 made possible the formation of compulsory cartels. On the motion of three-fourths of the firms in a particular industry, complete cartelization might be imposed on the entire industry. Apparently the big industrialists felt that this might make for too much bureaucratic control over their affairs. The law remained largely a dead letter.

244 mergers, comprising a capital of 13,000 million lire. At the end of 1929, one-fourth of the Italian stock companies controlled 86 per cent of the total corporate capital. By 1935, a quarter of the companies controlled 95 per cent of the capital. Forty-eight per cent of all stock-company capital was held by only 118 firms—that is, by half of one per cent of the total number of corporations. A Fascist official observed with satisfaction: 'The wealth of the few in whose hands capital is concentrated is also the wealth of the proletariat.' [5]

Cartels were formed in the iron and steel, shipbuilding, railway equipment, chemical, rayon, cement, and electric-light bulb industries. There also were numerous informal agreements for control of competitive practices. Powerful holding company systems arose. At the end of 1927 one electric-power holding company system controlled one-fourth of the power-producing capacity. In the field of chemicals, the *Montecatini* firm erected an almost complete monopoly. This concern, a special favorite of the Government, became one of the biggest chemical industries of the world, interested also in mining, metals, and electricity production. Semi-monopolistic organizations flowered also in the rayon, motor-vehicle, and iron and steel industries.

Moreover, management of the banks became more and more centralized and intimately connected with big industrial firms. Early in 1927 the Government brought about an amalgamation of smaller banking concerns, which extinguished over a hundred institutions. It also made the establishment of new banks subject to its control. The bigger banks were closely related, through interlocking directorates, with the management of manufacturing and commercial enterprises. In 1929, the directors of the four leading commercial banks held 149 seats on the boards of other banks and 1,510 directorates in 839 industrial companies. These firms comprised two-thirds of all the capital of Italian stock companies.

During the years of depression the State increasingly intervened in the financing of industry, and, at least indirectly, in the shaping of major business policies. This involved a reorganization of the banking system and assumption by the Government of the role of active supplier of loan funds in the capital markets. It also took the form of direct State subventions and premiums to especially distressed branches of industry and agriculture. Big business, unable to sell profitably in the impoverished private markets, found outlets opened to it by governmental public-works and armaments programs. For some industries the Government became virtually the only customer. Furthermore, the governmental machinery for control of the workers was useful to cut labor costs in the interests of business enterprise. An English student of Fascism stated approvingly: 'In no other country was it so easy to obtain the consent of the employees for a reduction of wages, in accordance with the fall in prices and the depressed state of industries.' [6]

The private banks were practically eliminated from direct participation in industrial and long-term financing. During the boom they had made huge investments in industrial company shares. Private savers in Italy had long preferred investments in Government bonds and bank deposits to direct purchases of industrial securities. Thus the bigger commercial banks had come to supply not only operating capital, but also much capital for investment in fixed assets such as plant and equipment. The decline of company earnings and stock prices after 1926 placed these banks in a dangerously illiquid situation. The two biggest institutions, indeed, were near suspension. The capital markets were at a practical standstill. To rescue the banks from serious losses on their private security investments, the Government intervened repeatedly. But it required that they limit themselves thereafter to short-term, fluid loans. In November 1931 it established a liquidating corporation that took over from the big banks large blocks of industrial securities. This Corporation issued securities backed by the public credit, raised some 4,000 million lire and placed this at the disposal of the banks in return for their industrial investments.

The financial structure of a number of large industrial enterprises also showed signs of severe strain after 1929. Here too the remedy was financial assistance from the Government. Several State-controlled agencies were set up in 1931 and 1933 for the purpose of reorganizing and financing overcapitalized companies. The capital of industrial firms was reduced, and their new issues were underwritten by these State organizations. Furthermore, a number of credit agencies were either established or enlarged (certain of them antedated Fascism) to operate in special fields, notably in the financing of public utilities, agricultural reclamation, public-works projects, shipping, and shipbuilding. These were all Government-controlled associations providing long-term funds, and issuing bonds supported by the Government. Their function was to cover private losses with governmental subventions. This was socialization of a kind, a socialization of business losses and risks. *

Italy thus was equipped with State and semi-State institutions that relieved the old banks of the function of financing fixed capital. The new lending agencies were responsible to

---

* It is interesting to note that the organs of the corporative system—the syndicates and the National Council of Corporations—played no formal role at all in the establishment of the refinancing agencies.

the Government with respect not only to their administration but also their purposes, and on their boards sat a majority of directors appointed by the Government. Their funds came in part from direct Government subsidies, but more largely from bond issues taken up by the social-insurance agencies and the savings banks. In effect, they were converting the people's savings into long-term industrial loans, guaranteed by the State. It was suggested that these institutions, with their control of a rather sizable portion of industrial capital, would be in a position to develop an increasing measure of outright State control of business management. No doubt certain of the 'syndicalist' Fascists wished this. But nothing of the sort took place—for the time being. Rather, the institutions were, as described by Mussolini, 'convalescent homes . . . whose expenses are met by the State.' [7]

In the field of foreign trade, the exigencies of depression also called forth much Government intervention. The currency stabilization and the subsequent deflation dealt a heavy blow to the export industries. This resulted not only from relatively high costs in Italy and decreased purchasing power abroad, but also from increasing competition by foreign industries selling in depreciated currencies. Italy's chief exports are fruits and vegetables, textiles, cheese, and a number of other specialties. These are all non-essential commodities, which may readily be dispensed with by foreign customers in times of depression. On the other hand, her imports consist principally of basic raw materials, which she largely or entirely lacks—coal, fuel, oils, wood pulp, raw cotton and wool, metals, and (in decreasing measure) cereals. These commodities are vital to the country's economy. Moreover, Italy for many years has had a considerable excess of imports over exports, the balance being provided largely by income from tourist and emigrant remittances. That is, in a period of world depression Italian industry found it very difficult to cut its imports, whereas its customers abroad could easily curtail their purchases.

After 1929 Italy's exports and imports declined about equally, and the excess of imports was maintained. But the balancing items—remittances, tourist expenditure, sales of shipping services—shrank drastically. The continued and even growing surplus of imports imposed a severe strain on Italian foreign exchange, led to an outward drain of gold and a serious threat to the stability of the lira. The minimum 40 per cent gold reserve behind note issues of the Bank of Italy was approached in the spring of 1934. It was deemed essential, then, to bring about a sharp reduction of imports. The Government took steps to limit imports drastically and to control the currency exchanges. All foreign securities and credits held by Italians had to be exchanged for State bonds.

Tariffs on imports were successively raised—in part as retaliation against foreign tariffs on Italian goods—and by 1935 Italy had one of the highest tariff walls in the world. The general level of rates in 1933 (in terms of 1914 gold lire) was estimated to be 185 per cent above that in 1914; but allowing for the decline of prices it was 274 per cent higher. For many goods the duties were prohibitive. Agreements for direct barter of certain commodities were also made with a number of countries. But the conventional tariff device was insufficient to control imports. Beginning in early 1934 a system of rigid quota control was developed in order to reduce to a minimum the purchases of non-essential goods abroad. By 1935 licenses were required for the importation of some 1,500 commodities. Under governmental supervision, various branches of industry pooled their purchases of foreign commodities. These measures, together with the controls of foreign exchange, gave the Government a practically complete command over all import trade. The required curtailment of imports was confined almost entirely to foodstuffs and finished manufactured goods, and had little effect on raw materials. The Government undertook to encourage exports by paying subsidies to exporters of especially depressed commodities. Furthermore, an agency was set up to improve marketing methods and quality of a number of important agricultural exports.

During the depression the Government also made direct subsidies to certain other propertied interests. It lent public funds to producers of iron, steel, and chemicals. Various debt-lightening measures—including low-cost loans, reduction of interest rates, participation in interest payments—were adopted to save landowners. Rice growers were aided by a subsidization of their exports, the funds for which were obtained from increased prices paid by Italian rice consumers. Bounties were paid to raw silk producers, manufacturers, and exporters. Increased public-works expenditures, too, provided an outlet for domestic industries. By the end of 1932 more than 8,500 million lire had been paid out to help depressed industries. How much more was advanced thereafter is uncertain.

In taxation matters, the regime—during its first years, at least—showed a remarkable solicitude for the propertied and entrepreneurial classes. Conveniently buried was the Fascist demand of 1919 for 'a heavy, extraordinary, progressive tax on capital that should have the form of a real partial expropriation of all wealth.' After the March on Rome a fiscal policy of this sort was dubbed by the Fascist Minister of Finance as 'infected with madness.' [8] It was decided that taxes must be levied so as to increase State revenues, and yet safeguard private wealth and encourage accumulation of capital. Accordingly, taxes on landed property and on business traffic were lightened, real estate assessment values were revised in such a way as to favor big landlords, the tax on family inheritances was abolished. At the same time, the tax base was broadened, and direct and indirect levies on the incomes of rural and urban workers were raised.

However, as the economic crisis deepened and the bureaucrats' power swelled, the wealthy came to be squeezed more and more. The burden of taxation rose markedly: it amounted to 13 per cent of the national income in 1914, 20 per cent in 1926, and at least 29 per cent in 1933. But much of this increase was eased off capital and shifted to the lower and middle classes. Because of heavy regressive sales taxes, customs duties and the levies of governmental sales monopolies—falling on even such common necessities as salt, sugar, and bread—the poor contributed a larger proportion of their incomes than did the rich. By 1932, 60 per cent of the Government's revenues were obtained from direct or indirect duties on consumption, as against 40 per cent coming from taxes on income and capital. Perhaps as much as three-fifths of the national tax revenues were extracted from the poor. On the whole, the burdens of supporting the State were distributed with gross unfairness.

This would not have been so serious if the low-income population had received increased benefits from the Government. But expenditures for education and social services were very small in comparison with huge and ever-increasing outlays for military and police purposes. Annual real governmental expenditures in 1930–33 were at least twice as large as at the beginning of the Fascist era. This increase was largely a result of the subventions of business and expenditures for

public works and armaments. Ten times as much as before
the war was being spent for police activities. But revenues
could not keep pace with the mounting costs of government.
In consequence, the State's budget showed continuous large
deficits after 1930. The national debt rose steadily. In 1934
it was estimated to be 50 per cent greater than in 1922.

To be sure, the men of property have had to pay dearly for
such favors as they have received from the Fascist hierarchy.
The official and quasi-official bureaucracy of course increased
in numbers, and—more important—in its interference with
the processes of business enterprise. The new Fascist politicians were in power primarily to serve their own interests,
not those of the magnates. Besides the compulsory levies of the
syndicates, business men have been forced to make large
'voluntary' contributions to the Party and to its subsidiary
organizations. According to some Fascist commentators,
these informal dues amount to almost as much as the regular
levies. Moreover, the promotion of friendly relations with
powerful officials has become more and more essential to
business survival. Insignificant business men who cannot
make the necessary connections are likely to find fortune
turning away from them. The financial operations of numerous petty Fascist hierarchs have not always been above suspicion, and occasionally rumors of serious graft on the part of
sub-leaders have broken through the barriers of censorship.

However, the heavy charges for supporting the army of
State and Party officials have been advertised as an insurance
against less happy conditions. When in 1934 there was some
grumbling among landlords in the Chamber of Deputies
against a proposed extension of State controls, the Minister
of Agriculture (himself a big landowner) admonished them
by pointing out that, after all, 'while nearly everywhere else

private property was bearing the major burdens and suffering from the hardest blows of the depression, in Italy, thanks to the action of the Fascist Government, private property not only has been saved, but has also been strengthened.' [9] About the same time another high official put it more dramatically: 'We are so little against property that one of the fundamental characteristics of our agricultural policy is to make the disinherited also property owners, and the corporate system certainly is not state socialism. . . . This ought above all to reassure those who fear that the Corporate State is a kind of Trojan horse in the citadel of private property, a horse whose inhabitants are the leaders of the workers' syndicates.' [10]

But it was a relatively small group of industrial firms, banks, and landlords that obtained the bulk of the State's aid. The Government certainly did not help all business men and landowners. Thousands of smaller manufacturers and merchants unable to obtain subsidies or loans were forced to go into bankruptcy (there were nearly 100,000 business failures during 1926–35, as compared with 28,000 in the preceding ten years). Among the landowners, it was a few large proprietors who were the main beneficiaries of loans. It was hinted, indeed, that individuals who had close personal relations with the Government were granted inordinate favors. Small farmers and peasants received little or no help; thousands of requests for financial aid were ignored by the Government. In 1934 a cabinet minister exclaimed (perhaps with exaggeration): 'Three-quarters of the landowners are effectively in the hands of the banks,' and added that every proprietor must be 'lighting a candle every hour to Saint Benito [Mussolini] with the prayer that he might one fine day absolve them of their debts, or at least their interest payments.' [11] And, as an Italian newspaper has pointed out, 'the great majority of rural wage-workers are frequently obliged by the needs of their families to borrow from local shopkeepers at not exactly philanthropic rates of interest.'

By 1934, according to Mussolini, fully three-quarters of Italian business rested on the shoulders of the State. [12] But he could have been referring only to banking and heavy industry. Signor Pirelli, an outstanding business man and a power in the corporative system, explained: 'Beyond the frontiers there has been a misunderstanding of the meaning of one of Mussolini's phrases to the effect that three-quarters of the Italian economic system, both industrial and agricultural, is under State supervision. Almost all the medium-sized and little firms and the great majority of slightly larger firms, with the exception of a few categories, are completely outside the sphere of the State's healing activity.' [13] Business policies came to be increasingly shaped by the Government, but security against the risks of business was provided only to the biggest capitalists.

Yet in their speeches and articles the Fascist leaders claimed not to have forgotten the importance of small business men, traders, and artisans. Guiseppe Bottai wrote in 1929: 'We must foster the growth and the concrete success of the small craftsmen, especially in order to prevent the progressive concentration of capital.' [14] 'Turning to small business, to that of the craftsmen and the manufacturer,' said Mussolini in 1936, 'I wish to make clear that the craftsman will be assisted. . . . We protect him, not only out of respect for a glorious tradition, but also in view of his effective value. Small- and medium-sized industry will remain the area of private enterprise and private responsibility, coordinated for national and social purposes by the self-imposed discipline of the Corporations.' [15] It is interesting to see how the Fascist Corporations undertook to 'co-ordinate' private enterprise 'for national and social purposes.'

The organization of twenty-two 'category corporations,' early in 1934, was acclaimed by Fascist politicians and economists as a bold step towards the realization of the corporative ideal. Now finally, individual economic interests were to be subordinated to national welfare. Mussolini announced that the Corporations were to be 'the instrument that, under the aegis of the State, carries out completely, organically, and in the general interest, the regulation of the productive forces, with a view to the expansion of the wealth, the political power, and the well-being of the Italian people. . . . It is essential that the institutions we have set up should, at a given moment, be felt and perceived by the masses themselves as the means by which the masses may improve their standard of life.' [16] But the powers legally bestowed on the Corporations were so uncertain as to give rise to widely divergent interpretations. Even after the Corporate State had been in existence for seven years, Mussolini could still ask (in November 1933): 'What functions ought the Corporations to perform? How many of them should there be? How should they be constituted?' [17] Certain more sanguine observers saw the new bodies as media for complete governmental control of the productive system, thus beginning a type of planned, collective economy. But this 'bolshevistic' view was contradicted by more powerful authorities, who looked upon the Corporations as useful auxiliaries to the going order. Thus, Professor Gino Arias—writing in the Duce's *Popolo d'Italia*—argued that 'one must first and foremost exclude the State or any public body such as a syndicate, or more important still a Corporation, from taking upon itself the management of businesses and thus elimi-

nating private enterprise or placing it in a thoroughly subordinate position. This would be in contradiction to the
Charter of Labor.' [18] Mussolini noted: 'Far too many pseudo-
philosophers have entered into lengthy discussions on the
Corporations, succeeding only in creating a muddle and
rendering abstruse the simplest of ideas.' [19]

The staffing and the actual work of the Corporations did
not suggest the impending doom of the traditional system of
business enterprise. The members of their governing councils
were eminently 'safe' personalities. Even theoretically they
were given no independent authority. They were merely to
recommend measures to the regular agencies of the Government, which remained free to act as it chose.

The numerous recommendations made by the Corporations could hardly be interpreted as pointing towards an
integrated control of the economy for the purpose of developing the 'well-being of the Italian people.' For the most
part, the Corporations were interested in promoting the
special interests of their business-minded constituents. To
the accompaniment of congratulatory addresses, they pe-
titioned the Government to restrict competitive imports
still further, to subsidize market-control plans, to support
profitable prices. Various Corporations, for example, asked
for wider use of Italian motors in fishing vessels, promotion
of Italian dress fashions, reduction of railway rates for particular goods, further aid to exporters of fruits and vegetables,
tariff protection for the tunny-fishing industry, higher duties
on lumber imports, conversion of the Bank of Italy into a
public institution, development of uniform market standards
for cheeses, wines, and textiles. Little attention was given to
problems of workers and consumers. All this was essentially
the ordinary behavior of business pressure-groups. An Ameri-

can observer reported that the business-minded members of the Corporation councils 'consulted and came to agreements on matters of common concern probably in the same manner as they had been accustomed to do in the past and would do in the future outside the institutional framework of a governmental body. Some of their mutual arrangements now took the form of regulations sanctioned by the State and probably in return they took some actions through political considerations.' [20] No doubt the Corporations were useful in supplying technical information and advice to the regular economic departments of the Government. But they represented no serious modification of the existing economy. If that were to come, it would be outside the operations of the business traffic of the Corporations.

Thus Fascist intervention in economic affairs benefited a few men of big business and landed property and the governing hierarchy. The vested interests of great industrialists and landlords were maintained and strengthened. Profits remained private, and only the losses of the favorites were socialized. The masses of the people—their old defenses destroyed—could make the most of the glory of their rulers.

But there was little originality in the devices of the emerging Corporate State. In form it was a bureaucratic structure fitted over the framework of the old order. In behavior it was hardly different from other mechanisms through which powerful interest groups demand and get favors in the name of national honor and integrity and well-being. As a student of the Corporate State wrote: 'The control of the Italian economy belongs to the oligarchy of the great employers' confederations, but in a dictatorial regime the bearing of politics and administration upon private activity is so profound that Fascism has been able to give the impression of securing a control over the Italian economy which, in fact, escapes it.' [21] Another observer declared: 'So far, the new Corporative State only amounts to the establishment of a new and costly bureaucracy from which those industrialists who can spend the necessary amount can obtain almost anything they want, and put into practice the worst kind of monopolistic practices at the expense of the little fellow who is squeezed out in the process.' [22]

Yet despite the efforts of the Fascist regime to salvage property interests and promote recovery, Italy was in an unhappy condition at the end of 1934. For, after more than ten years of power, Fascism had been unable to solve Italy's economic difficulties. Mussolini was forced to admit: 'We touched bottom some time ago. We shall go no farther down. Perhaps it would be hard to sink any lower. . . . We are probably moving towards a period of humanity resting on a lower standard of living. We must not be alarmed at the prospect. Humanity is capable of asceticism such as we perhaps cannot conceive.' [23] Not long after, in inaugurating the Corporations, he announced: 'One must not expect miracles.' [24] Industrial production remained at low ebb, foreign trade still fell off, unemployment was at a distressingly high level and efforts to combat it had had little substantial effect. All this was very harmful to Fascist prestige.

Continued economic troubles and the inner pressures of Fascism impelled the Dictatorship to seek escape in foreign fields. War might be a kind of public works vastly more effective in reviving industry than anything tried before. With their attention focused on the glories of the battlefield, the people might be diverted from an uncomfortable concern over their domestic misfortunes. And certainly a military victory would solidify the Fascist movement and restore its fading glamour.

In this crisis, the rulers themselves would learn that the machine they had built—under whose dominion men must live in constant spiritual tension, in fear and uncertainty—is above all an engine of warlike enterprise.

# VII : THE POWER OF THE SWORD

THE Fascist legions crossed the Abyssinian frontiers early in October 1935. A few weeks later the League of Nations applied 'economic sanctions' against Italy. These sanctions consisted of the suspension by fifty-two nations of commodity imports from Italy, and a prohibition of commercial credits and the export of important raw materials (not including petroleum, however) to that country. The professed aim was to force Italy to give up the attack on Abyssinia by cutting off her ability to obtain abroad supplies necessary to her army and people.

Mussolini no doubt was at first annoyed and worried by the sanctions program. But soon he found it to be an extraordinary stroke of luck. No great popular enthusiasm for the African adventure had developed in Italy during the summer and early autumn in 1935. There was much grumbling and even unpleasant signs of outright opposition among the rank and file of the people. Many business men and military experts had misgivings about the sanity of such a war. The sanctions, however, gave the Dictator an opportunity to arouse a tremendous moral indignation and patriotic fervor among the Italians. An unsavory colonial campaign was turned into a sacred defense of the homeland against the evil forces of rich and selfish foreign powers. It was 'proletarian Italy against the World.'

The half-hearted imposition of sanctions, instead of sapping Italy's military strength, actually intensified her effort to win a rapid victory. She had considerable reserves of arms and

137

other war materials, and the one embargo that could have embarrassed her vitally—that on petroleum—was never put into effect. Governmental controls over foreign trade and prices—already established in the preceding years of depression—were extremely useful in retaliating against the sanctionist trade restrictions and in directing the Italian economy along the paths of war. Given more time, even the partial sanctions might ultimately have upset Mussolini's calculations. But the reluctance of the Great Powers to take more determined steps to halt the war, their fine impartiality in denying arms both to aggressor and victim, the enormous military superiority of the Italian forces, were a guarantee of victory for Fascism. Sanctions failed because of the speed with which the Abyssinians were overwhelmed, the aid that Italy obtained from non-sanctionist powers, the military effectiveness of totalitarian controls, and the widespread moral support that the Dictatorship won at home. The capture of Addis Ababa signalled a remarkable triumph—economic and diplomatic—for Fascism and for Mussolini personally. His position at home was immensely strengthened.

Happily for Italian business, the war brought about a measure of industrial revival. The sanctions injured certain export trades, to be sure. But the output of other branches of industry was stimulated by Government purchases of war supplies and increased sales to private consumers cut off from foreign markets. Industrial production in 1935 was more than fifteen per cent greater than in 1934, and it continued to rise during 1936-7. Unemployment declined by several hundred thousands in the spring of 1935 because of the rise in business activity and military mobilization. The Government's prohibition of corporation dividends in excess of six per cent of capital stock during the period of the war apparently was no damper on business enterprise. Profits rose considerably: total net earnings of all stock companies were 2.9 per cent of capital in 1934, 5.1 per cent in 1935, 6.6 per cent in 1936, 7.2 per cent in 1937.

The Abyssinian war was advertised to the Italian people as a conquest of land and labor for the masses. League sanctions were portrayed as an attempt on the part of 'capitalist' powers to prevent 'proletarian' Italy from winning her just share of the world's riches. The Fascist rationale was that Italy had received no addition to her economic resources at the end of the World War, although she had done more than any other nation to insure the Allies' victory, that emigration outlets for Italians had been almost completely closed, that trade restrictions abroad had cut off Italian export markets. The doctrines of exasperated nationalism, economic self-sufficiency, and manipulated currencies prevailed, and Italy had no choice but to resort to similar measures in self-defense. The regime was merely showing the hungry people of Italy the road to a new promised land. Conquered Abyssinia was to give land, bread, and liberty to the Italians. At the end of the campaign it was announced by the Government that Italy was 'now a satisfied country, able and willing to be a strong factor for peace and stability in Europe and the world.' [1]

Joint business and Government organizations were set up immediately for exploitation of the new possession, and plans for its development were projected. It appeared that the Government would make a show of peasant colonization by subsidizing a limited number of settlers in the few favorable regions of the country. But enormous military, climatic, and economic difficulties stood in the way of extensive peasant settlement. In August 1937 the Fascist colonial minister wrote: 'In regions where European workers cannot be settled there will be opportunity, by means of concessions, for the formation of agricultural plantations worked by native labor.' This sounded like an admission that much of Abyssinia cannot be developed by individual Italian peasants and workers, but only by capitalistic enterprises. Land certainly will be taken from the natives, but its control and its fruits in all probability will pass into the hands of a privileged minority of big concessionaries, colonization and plantation companies, and financial institutions.

As the months passed, the dream of immense riches to be found in Abyssinia began to dissipate. Two years after the fall of Addis Ababa, the Italians had established military domination of the few large towns and the main roads, but elsewhere their control was still precarious. A 'corporative' system of economic regulation had been transplanted precipitately, yet was apparently not producing the desired results. Exports from Abyssinia had come to a virtual standstill, whereas imports of goods needed by the large forces of occupation had increased tremendously. The natives were engaging in passive resistance, and guerilla warfare continued in outlying regions. As a result, troops could not be withdrawn in substantial numbers. Production had not returned to the pre-war level, and living costs soared. While much was said about large-scale colonization, little progress was actually made. The alleged vast mineral wealth of Abyssinia remained to be discovered.

A most significant result of the Abyssinian affair was the Fascist regime's adoption of a policy of extreme economic nationalism, designed to 'free Italy from foreign economic servitude.' This of course did not originate wholly with the sanctions experience. In a fundamental sense, it is another legacy of the World War and the fears, hatreds, and mistrust that it had aroused. Self-sufficiency in foodstuffs had become one of the avowed goals of the regime with the initiation of the Battle of Wheat in 1925. In order to reduce coal imports, the Government had long since encouraged hydro-electric power production. But the potential menace of the sanctions drove home a realization of Italy's vulnerability to a really determined blockade. To prepare for war, then, Italy must at all cost secure a maximum of economic autonomy. Another consideration, perhaps, was the benefit that certain industrial interests stood to win through a further elimination of imports from Italian markets. Important, too, was a desire to reduce the chronically unfavorable balance of trade and to conserve foreign exchange.

The keynote of the new departure was given by the Duce in March 1936: 'Political independence—that is, the possibility of pursuing an independent foreign policy—cannot be conceived without a corresponding capacity for economic self-sufficiency. . . . We must secure in the shortest possible time the maximum degree of economic independence for the nation. . . . This plan is dominated by one premise—the inevitability of war. When? How? No one can say, but the wheel of destiny turns quickly.' [2]

This challenge was immediately echoed in the official ranks. Edmondo Rossoni, now Minister of Agriculture, explained to the Chamber of Deputies that 'autarchy will leave much gold in our hands that otherwise would go abroad. It will be quite useless for people to say that everything that costs less abroad ought to be imported. We must pay gold for our imports, whereas everything we produce at home calls for that much more Italian labor paid in Italian money. (Applause)' [3] The people were told that 'proletarian' Italy needs a greater share of the world's resources. But only a fully-armed Italy can win respect from the 'plutocratic' nations. And military power demands economic independence.

Autarchy necessitates State control over imports and over indispensable raw materials to see that they are used 'rationally'—that is, in accordance with military and political purposes. It also involves an attempt to restrict imports to countries within easy reach in case of war. Finally, it means development of a variety of commodities in Italy that can be substituted, regardless of cost, for as many imported basic goods as possible. The elaborate mechanism of controls over foreign trade and the exchanges, built up originally to protect currency stability, was well suited to the promotion of this program.

New industrial processes using substitute materials were subsidized. In early 1938 it was reported that output of low-grade domestic coal, iron ore, aluminum, dye-stuffs, and paper was steadily rising. Moderately good results were being obtained in the production of *lanital*, a synthetic wool made from milk casein. But its output was limited by the small animal population of Italy. Rayon and hemp were being substituted for wool, cotton, and jute fibers. The liquid fuel problem was being tackled by refinement of the poor Albanian crude oil, distillation of domestic lignites, and the mixing of alcohol—made from beets, rice, and wine—with gasoline. Castor oil was used to some extent in place of other oils for motor lubrication. Progress was also made in producing cadmium as a substitute for copper. Wheat straw was yielding cellulose and paper stock. Plants for the production of synthetic nitrates were being enlarged, and the electrification of the railways made considerable headway. By the end of 1937 nearly a quarter of the railway mileage was electrified.

The mechanical industries were converted to a war-time

basis and placed almost entirely at the service of the military forces. For example, the biggest typewriter firm in the country turned to the production of machine guns. The automobile industry concentrated on making army trucks, tanks, cannon, and aeroplanes. The war-frenzied State became the main or only customer of other industries, too. Many factories—especially those producing armaments—were placed under governmental surveillance, their buildings guarded by soldiers and their workers subjected to military discipline. Capital for the new enterprises and equipment was supplied largely by the quasi-State credit agencies. This enabled the Government to play an increasingly significant part in the managerial policies of large-scale industrial concerns.

In other directions, too, the range of governmental controls was extended. Foreign trade became an instrument for carrying out the policies of the State. During the period of currency deflation the Party—through provincial and national committees—had attempted to regulate retail prices of a number of staples. In 1936 and 1937 price-fixing was extended to many other commodities, and its administration was transferred to the Central Corporative Committee. Its main effort was directed toward checking the rise in living costs. The Corporations were also entrusted with authority over wage rates, the distribution of import quotas, plant expansion, and industrial investments. Early in 1936 unified governmental control over the entire banking and financial system was established. Thereafter, the credit agencies were required to advance their funds as directed by the Government. Thus mastery over the nation's loan-capital resources was concentrated in the hands of the State. The corporative institutions seemed to be evolving, not into agencies of the promised new economic order, but into the tools of a sovereign political and economic bureaucracy.

War and preparation for more war—the pacification and development of Abyssinia, intervention in the Spanish civil war, autarchy and armaments—added new burdens on the shoulders of taxpayers of all classes. In 1934 Mussolini granted that taxation had reached a prohibitive level: 'I am the first to declare that the pressure of taxation has attained the limit, and that the Italian taxpayer must be given a breathing space of absolute tranquillity; if possible, his burden must be lightened.' [4] Given the policies on which the regime was embarking, it was impossible to fill this prescription. On the contrary, additional revenues had to be attained.

New taxes were improvised, and old ones increased. Heavier duties were levied on consumption of gasoline, textiles, cotton, coal, electricity, and on road transport. Railway rates were advanced. The sales tax was raised, and new duties on legal paper and business transactions were introduced. But the wage-earning and salaried classes were already staggering under the weight of direct and indirect taxation—it was said that taxes were absorbing at least 35 per cent of the national income. It was necessary to adopt extraordinary measures to put additional purchasing power in the hands of the Government. In June 1935 tenants of houses in the larger towns and cities were required to buy State securities in proportion to their rentals. (These securities were to be held, not by the tenants, but by the landlords as a security for prompt payment of rent!) The Government had to knock at the doors of the propertied for more funds. During the period of the Abyssinian war payment of stock-company dividends greater than 6 per cent was prohibited, and excess profits had to be invested in State bonds. In the autumn of 1936 this measure was replaced by a heavy tax on dividends. At the same time, owners of real estate were forced to subscribe to Government bonds in the amount of 5 per cent of the value of their property. A year later a 10 per cent capital levy was imposed on the capital and reserves of joint-stock companies —a type of taxation that only shortly before had been called 'demagogic' by the finance minister. The companies might elect to pay this tax by yielding up part of their shares to the Government, thus enlarging the stake that it already held in industrial enterprises. Late in 1938, the Government resorted to another levy—this time on the capital of commercial and industrial enterprises other than joint-stock companies. These levies were justified by the Government as merely a means of insuring participation by the Treasury in the increased nominal values of property resulting from lira devaluation, and were, therefore, not confiscatory. The finance minister proudly declared that such measures could take place 'only in a disciplined nation, whose citizens have a mature tax conscience.' [5] Consistent with this development— and perhaps unpleasantly suggestive to all proprietors—was the Government's decision at the end of 1938 to expropriate the major real-estate and business holdings of Italian Jews.

The new taxes, together with rising business activity, served to increase State revenues, but not nearly enough to meet the huge expenditures for armaments and for the campaigns in Abyssinia and Spain. 'The conquest and development of the Empire and the needs of the defence services' cost at least 38,000 million lire in 1934–8, [6] and 3,000 millions were said to have been advanced to the Spanish rebels in 1936–7.* Therefore the Government borrowed still more,

---

* Outlays for military purposes amounted to about 45 per cent of total Government expenditures in 1936–7.

and the national debt rose by about one-third during 1934–8. The State was said to be taking at least a quarter of the national savings, much of which it was using unproductively. This was a loss of capital that Italy could ill afford. Deficit financing was facilitated by the quasi-State insurance and credit institutions, which stood ready to invest the funds under their control in governmental debentures, and also by the considerable coercion of private savers to turn their money over to the State.

The totalitarian State showed itself more capable than the liberal and parliamentary regimes in pressing income out of its people. Low wage rates—in the face of increasing employment and production—yielded large savings in labor costs, which ordinarily would have augmented profits. But the heavy taxes diverted these savings into State revenues. At the same time, the throttling of consumption reduced the demand for private investments, and enlarged the supply of capital available to the State. The limit of State expenditures was set by the lowest depth to which the real income of the masses could be driven. The Government was fortunate in that the frugal Italian people could be made to accept even lower living standards.

The fiscal situation was difficult enough to give rise to persistent rumors that the Government was seeking to place loans abroad. Officials denied this, and insisted that Italy could carry on alone. However, they declared that Italy would welcome private capital seeking a 'safe place of refuge.' Special tax concessions were offered to foreign investors, but apparently there was little response. Even heavier taxes—including more capital levies—seemed to be in prospect.

The nation's material wealth has diminished under the strain of autarchy. Huge outlays for armaments may yield profits to certain industries. But they are an appalling burden on the slender Italian economy. Normal, peace-time industrial plant and equipment have been wearing down. Funds that would ordinarily be invested in consumer-goods industries were directed by the Government into a one-sided development of the war industries. Reserves of wheat, rubber, oil, gold, and other metals fell. The comparative neglect of the non-military industries led to a shortage of some commodities. Prices rose, despite the attempts at Government control. Every endeavor was made to regain the export markets and to increase tourist traffic. The effort to maintain the lira at the level set in 1927 was finally abandoned in October 1936. (It was devalued to a point that placed it in about the same position relative to foreign currencies that it had occupied before 1931.) Currency depreciation for a time yielded some advantages to the export trades. But as domestic costs of production rose, these advantages vanished. The prices of imported goods, needed in larger volume by the armaments industries, advanced more than the prices of Italian exports. Poor wheat crops required large-scale purchases of foreign cereals. (This, together with the need to safeguard wheat stocks against the danger of war, led to the adulteration of bread—at least the bread of the poor—by adding maize and other vegetable matter to wheat flour.) Therefore, although imports were strictly rationed, the unfavorable balance of trade mounted.* In 1938, with the decline of raw-material prices in world markets, there was some improvement in the Italian balance.

---

* The merchandise deficit in 1937 was 5,640 million lire, higher than any since 1929. This was partially offset by an estimated income of 2,500 millions from tourism, emigrant remittances, and shipping services. The Government insisted that its gold and exchange reserves had been maintained without loss during 1937. To what extent the balance of 3,140 millions was met by capital imports and liquidation of foreign investments held by Italians could not be ascertained.

According to reasonable standards of economic soundness and popular welfare, autarchy is a ruinous policy. Complete self-sufficiency is, of course, impossible for the existing Italian economy. Even to move partially toward that goal, however, calls for expensive investments in machinery and plant, investments that would better go into fields of production in which Italy has a comparative advantage over other countries. Moreover, autarchy reduces the flow of international trade, and narrows still further the Italian export opportunities.

Italy's poverty in capital and natural resources make economic nationalism highly undesirable. The Italians cannot raise enough food to feed themselves, although the country is largely agricultural. The paucity of coal and iron and other basic raw materials hampers the heavy industries with relatively high production costs. In a rational world economy, the material well-being of the Italians would be served by opportunities for emigration, and by an exchange of their fruits and vegetables, wines and cheeses, textiles and glass, their scenic, climatic, and cultural riches, for the wheat, cotton, and machinery of other peoples. International peace, freedom of trade and migration, would be of especial advantage to Italy. The intrusion of non-rational factors into the world order, for which the Fascist regime is by no means entirely responsible, have made this impossible. But Fascism itself is the most cruel evidence of the perversion of reason.

More sober minds in the governing ranks have been aware of these difficulties. Felice Guarneri, the foreign-exchange minister, explained that 'autarchy in the Fascist corporative sense does not mean a complete cutting of trade relations with other countries and withdrawal into absolute isolation. Economic autonomy—in times of peace—must be more potential than actual.' [7] That is, the policy is understandable solely as a preparation for war.

The standard of living of the masses has fallen, yet the people are ordered to prepare for 'new and greater sacrifices.' Fascist extremists hold that rational economic standards should not be applied to the program of autarchy. Rossoni has pointed out: 'There are those who assert that this or that production is uneconomical, because it costs more to make at home than to import it. Once and for all a stop must be put to this attitude of pure money-making and business accounting.' [8] Others say: 'We are suffering from the maladies of growth. . . . We must lower present standards for the good of the future. . . . Only by growing stronger shall we attain a fuller life. . . . Our revolution signifies the rise of working classes and the re-distribution of wealth.' [9] The people are told, in schools and newspapers, that Italy won the World War, but was given only a few crumbs off the table of Versailles. Italy's economic troubles are the fault of the 'plutocratic' countries who have sought to crush the new authoritarian states and their peoples by means of economic, political, and moral blockade. To prevent suffocation, Italy must fight back. And this requires that she prepare for war, become self-sufficient in foodstuffs and military equipment, develop a great army, and whip up a fighting spirit. Eventually, the reward must come in a more abundant life for the Italians.

Nevertheless, discontent smoulders over wide sections of the population, not only among the long-suffering workers and peasants, but also among the middle classes. Whatever the future prizes, the present cost of the warlike policy is a further impoverishment of the people.

Autarchy and militarization no doubt have benefited certain big firms doing business with the State. The Government has even guaranteed minimum profits to some of the favored industries. It is widely complained that prosperity has been reserved for only a few of the large quasi-monopolies— *Montecatini, Fiat, Terni,* and others—which have close connections with the Government and thus are able to obtain State subsidies, contracts, and raw materials at favorable terms. Signor Guarneri declared frankly: 'In my opinion too many of our business firms find it convenient to live a sheltered life at home, under the protection of customs duties and of quotas, quietly seated at the table of the home market or relying on Government orders. . . .' [10]

But medium-sized and small business men, especially those producing goods for private consumption and those unable to get political privileges, fare badly. The furniture, glass, marble, clothing, and a host of other small industries—dependent upon mass purchasing power at home and abroad—have fallen into a state of near-ruin. Small merchants are caught between the upper and the nether millstones of monopolistic price-control. The uncertainties of the future arouse uneasiness among many enterprisers. To pay for the swollen bureaucracy that reaches out to regulate the affairs of business men themselves, tax payments, 'voluntary' contributions, and compulsory investments in State bonds are rising at the expense of profits. Stock-company net income in the two fiscal years 1935–6 was far higher than in any of the preceding five years. Yet 99.7 per cent of the companies got only about one-third of this revenue. The remainder went to the 56 biggest firms, which controlled about 40 per cent of all stock-company capital. The great trusts and war-industries—machinery, metals, sugar, chemical, electricity, and banking companies— gained, whereas the consumer-goods and export industries—

notably cotton and silk textile, clothing, fishing, shipping, and quarrying firms—suffered losses.*

Some of the big industrialists even are not wholly satisfied. For politics is assuming a primacy over business. They are restrained from investing their money abroad or at home as they please. Instead, they must sink their surplus funds in governmental securities or in dubious plant expansions, as directed by the political necessities of the State. Governmental intervention in foreign trade, investment, price-making, and the necessity of catering to the bureaucracy, raise the costs of business administration. The traditional leaders of enterprise are losing their grip on economic affairs. The crescendo of militarism is not to their liking, for its threat of war-to-come is noxious from the business standpoint. Agreeable or not, the martial policies of the State must be accepted. Perhaps capitalists realize that for them there is no alternative to Fascism.

In the autumn of 1937—shortly after the imposition of the levy on stock-company capital—Mussolini was obliged to take note of the dissatisfaction that was sweeping a large section of the business community. In his speech commemorating the fifteenth anniversary of the March on Rome, he declared that he had to smile at the reaction of 'so-called public opinion' to 'the logical, necessary and just financial measures the Fascist regime has adopted and that have been accepted with absolute discipline and understanding by the interested

---

* Output of the metallurgical and mechanical industries in 1937 was 30 per cent greater than in 1928, while production of the textile industries remained 16 per cent below its 1928 level. The great *Montecatini* combine (chemicals) earned net profits of 6.4 per cent of its nominal capital in 1936, and 9.9 per cent in 1937. Profits of *Fiat* (automobiles, tractors, motors, mechanical armaments), *Breda* (engineering), and *Snia Viscosa* (synthetic fibers) in 1937 were 14.4, 14.5, and 13.9 per cent, respectively, of their share capital.

parties. . . . We cannot be measured by such ridiculous standards. In Fascist Italy capital is at the State's orders. It is necessary to emigrate into other countries blessed by immortal principles to find the diametrically opposite phenomenon—a State prone to capital's order.' [11] These remarks —it should be noted—were for popular consumption. At that very time, however, the Ministry of Corporations published a summary of the Central Corporative Committee's proceedings, which concluded with the comforting assurance that 'self-sufficiency does not imply absorption into the State of industry, agriculture, commerce and credit, nor yet an integral nationalization of the most important enterprises on behalf of the national economy. On the contrary, Fascism, faithful to its own theory and practice, will continue to consider private enterprise as one of the most powerful instruments for the production of wealth and well-being. . . .' [12]

Among the masses of workers, peasants, small farmers, and shopkeepers—many of them by no means congenitally anti-Fascist—there is hushed criticism and grumbling. They have seen their incomes declining and their tax payments rise to appallingly high levels. They resent the favors shown to big industrialists and the high prices charged by the monopolies. Nor are the new empire and intervention in Spain nearly so popular as the Government has pretended. Italy is winning her place in the Roman sun, but the bread of the Italians is being adulterated. The glories of war are poor compensation for poverty. For example, the Lion of Judah was brought by the Fascists from Addis Ababa to Rome. One morning in the spring of 1938 a large lump of stale and poor bread was found tied around the lion's neck. On a piece of cardboard was written: 'It is you who gave us this bread, and you can eat it.' A widely circulated story contrasts Communism, Socialism, and Fascism: 'The Communists tell the peasant, "We will take all your cows from you"; the Socialists say, "We will take only half your cows; you may keep the others"; the Fascists, however, announce to the poor peasant, "You may keep your cows. But every day we will come and get all their milk." ' Having lost such political and cultural liberties as they formerly enjoyed, the people cannot even hold their own materially. Nor can they cherish the hope that present sacrifices must mean greater material welfare in the future. They live in a state of permanent emergency, and the only certainty that the future seems to hold is war.

Yet it appears that popular discontent is too inarticulate, too disorganized, to form a serious threat to the regime. There is nothing within the domestic situation that points to 'the inevitable collapse.' The Government protects itself with its vigilant police and intensive propaganda. Through its controls over the thoughts of the masses it holds the amorphous opposition in check. Its constant emotional appeals to the patriotic virtues, the identification of the regime with the faith and loyalties of the Italians, the martial parades and organized cheering, even result in giving an impression of popular enthusiasm for Fascism. Not least important is the personal fascination of the Duce. His has been the good fortune to win applause and to escape the censure that is thrown at his Government. Men might hate his lieutenants; criticize, condemn, and fear his works; and yet feel a deep loyalty to Mussolini himself. When the Duce shouts: 'Italy was offered the ridiculous alternative of butter or guns. We have made our choice. And what have we chosen?' he can be certain that the crowd in the market-place will roar back the proper answer: 'Guns! Guns!' [13]

The official picture portrays an Italian people 'animated

by the profound human aspirations that inspire the super-human, and at the same time so human, work of Benito Mussolini.' [14] The propaganda agents unceasingly thunder that Italy before 1922 was backward and weak, while everything that happened after the March on Rome is glorious, noble, unrivalled elsewhere. The people are told that they owe their troubles to the hostility of the rich and selfish Powers, and that at any rate conditions are better in Italy than in the outside world. Occasional well-timed, widely-advertised economic concessions are made to the lower classes, with the effect of giving a fillip to the common man's esteem for the Government. The cults of Nationalism and the Saviour-Leader—these are the mightiest of the weapons of Fascism.

Most tragic is the spiritual impoverishment of the country. Freedom of expression on any but quite harmless topics is impossible. No one may speak frankly except in closest privacy, and then only at risk. Freedom of thought even is a luxury not lightly to be indulged. Public opinion is made to order. Men of talent, whether in private or public life, have found that they are secure only if they are ready to descend into the roles of political sycophants. The ostentatious panegyric has taken the place of honest, critical judgment. Instead of genuine popular concern for the political life, there are only empty processions, meaningless shouts and gestures. The security of the *Passo del Brenner* has been given away, as wags say, in exchange for the '*Passo romano*,' that is, the goose-step. And the people applaud their own subjection. The result is a degrading hypocrisy and servility that permeate the whole society.

Intellectually, there can be little respect for the regime. Public office is to be won and held more by cultivating the habits of a lackey than by hard work and accomplishment.

Men who, for one reason or another, have once pledged their allegiance to Fascism, are obliged blindly to follow Mussolini wherever he may lead. Fascism is hardly an environment in which initiative and conscientious responsibility can flourish. Development of a self-reliant corps of administrators seems incompatible with the narrow oligarchy. What will happen to the body politic when the cohesive and stimulating energy of the Duce is gone? This is a question that many thoughtful men ask but no one ventures to answer.

The atmosphere of uniformity, suspicion, fear, adulation, buffoonery, and intellectual fawning are fatal to vigorous creative thought. Cultural life loses vitality and meaning. Scholarship, especially in the social sciences, is reduced to an exercise in platitudes and flattery. Rationalism yields before mystic stupidities; enlightenment is thwarted by the substitution of blind faith for critical skepticism. Racial superstitions and anti-Semitism, nurtured by the Government, begin to take root in an unwelcome Italian soil. Many intellectuals flee from present realities to the comforts of the past. The contemporary literature reflects a cynical and morbid pessimism. In no field of art has Fascism itself given the world anything of value. It is merely feeding on the glorious cultural traditions of Italy.

The youth are debauched by the rituals of hyper-nationalism and the deification of the Dictator. Their mentality is stunted. Insulated from the past and from ideas across the frontiers, they come to think of Fascist Rome as the shining center of the world. Their humanitarian impulses are undermined by the worship of sheer violence. When their hero speaks, it is in phrases such as these: 'Only in war do the fundamental virtues of man reveal themselves in the full light of day.' [15] The barracks, the parade ground, and—most exquisite of all—the aerial bomb, these must be their symbols of legitimate civilization. It can only be hoped that despite their teachings most young Italians are less insensitive than was the Duce's son, Vittorio, when he described his bombing of the miserable Abyssinians as 'exceptionally good fun.' For him, at least, war is 'the most beautiful and complete of all sports.'

The Fascists express only contempt for the ideals and tactics of democracy, liberalism, humanitarianism. They glorify war and the absolutism of the State. Withal they boldly assert that the Corporate State points to a new social order, which alone can offer salvation to the world. Mussolini has said: 'We can now assert that the capitalistic method of production has been superseded, and with it the theory of economic liberalism which illustrated and supplied the apology for it. . . . The Corporations supersede Socialism and liberalism; they create a new synthesis. . . . From both we inherit all that was vital.' [16] That is, only Fascism can solve the crisis of capitalism. Moreover, it must be the pattern for the European world: 'Today I hold that Fascism as an idea, a doctrine, a realization, is universal. . . . Therefore anyone may see a Fascist Europe drawing inspiration for her institutions from the doctrine and practice of Fascism.' [17]

Actually, Fascism has aggravated the basic difficulties of the old society. By annihilating the labor movement, it did succeed for a time in bolstering up the traditional economic order. But the Fascist hierarchy has exacted a heavy toll from the groups that called it to power. Like the Praetorian Guard, it can well threaten to impose its own will upon many of the older propertied classes. Its own inhumane creed and economic instability drive Italy towards an ever more aggressive foreign policy and towards war. And as martial activity mounts, the power of the hierarchy is exalted.

The words written by Thorstein Veblen in 1904 are prophetic. 'The direct cultural value of a warlike business policy is unequivocal. It makes for a conservative animus on the part of the populace. . . . The more consistent and the more comprehensive this military training, the more effectually will the members of the community be trained into habits of subordination and away from that growing propensity to make light of personal authority that is the chief infirmity of democracy. This applies first and most decidedly, of course, to the soldiery, but it applies only in a less degree to the rest of the population. They learn to think in warlike terms of rank, authority, and subordination, and so grow progressively more patient of encroachment upon their civil rights. . . . The modern warlike policies are entered upon for the sake of peace, with a view to the orderly pursuit of business. . . . But . . . the pomp and circumstance of war and armaments, the sensational appeals to patriotic pride and animosity made by victories, defeats, or comparisons of military and naval strength, act to rehabilitate lost ideals and weakened convictions of the chauvinistic or dynastic order. At the same stroke they direct the popular interest to other nobler, institutionally less hazardous matters than the unequal distribution of wealth or of creature comforts. . . . The warlike culture takes back to a more archaic situation that preceded the scheme of natural rights, viz. the system of absolute government, dynastic politics, devolution of rights and honors, ecclesiastical authority, and popular submission and squalor. . . . Loyal affections gradually shift from the business interests to the warlike and dynastic interests. . . . This may easily be carried so far as to sacrifice the profits of the business men to the exigencies of the higher politics. . . . The net outcome of the latter-day return to warlike enterprise is, no doubt, securely to be rated as fostering a reversion to national ideals of servile status and to institutions of a despotic character. . . . Authenticity and sacramental dignity belong neither with the machine technology, nor with modern science, nor with business traffic. In so far as the aggressive politics and the aristocratic ideals currently furthered by the business community are worked out freely, their logical outcome is an abatement of those cultural features that distinguish modern times from what went before, including a decline of business enterprise itself.'[18]

Under Fascism, Italy has remained a poor country—one of low income and restricted consumption—yet bearing an appallingly heavy burden of unproductive taxes. The land of *dolce far niente* has become the embodiment of Police State and Nation-in-Arms. Economically, it is developing into a closed system preparing for war. Its rulers—themselves swept along by forces they have unleashed—cry out like gamblers: 'When? How? No one can say, but the wheel of destiny turns quickly.' The principle of private ownership of the means of production is formally maintained. But industrial concentration and the increasingly pervasive influences of the bureaucracy have given a new aspect to the capitalist order. The controls over wealth are being concentrated as a result, not of technological progress, but of economic degradation. If profits have been restricted, this has been done not to advance social justice but to feed warlike appetites. Traditional class-distinctions measured by economic standards are fading. The proletariat have been reduced to impotence, and their living standards—always low—have been depressed still further. The middle classes of agriculture and the trades are also falling into ruin. Nor can even the rich feel quite secure. Indeed, pressure on proprietors as well as on workers is an essential of the quasi-war economy. Other elements of the old middle classes—the Party members who have risen from anonymity to positions of political authority—profit from the inflation of the State. This new parasitic group, establishing close personal ties with big business, penetrates more and more into the realms of property. Its power and its interests, however, are essentially political. The pseudo-philosophy of class-collaboration is but a mask over the face of its cancerous tyranny. Fascism has shown the world that despite economic decadence and the opposition of many of its subjects a dictatorship armed with modern weapons of persuasion and force can be maintained for a long time. Tyranny in the age of machines presages the triumph of power over reason.

Is Fascism the first shadow of a black night of Caesarism, inevitably descending over the Western World? It is for men everywhere to answer and to act.

# NOTES

THE sources of statistical data are with few exceptions the official documents of the Italian Central Statistical Office, chiefly its *Annuario Statistico Italiano*, published annually in Rome.

### CHAPTER I

1 Quoted by Rodolfo Morandi, *Storia della grande industria in Italia*, Bari 1931, p.173.

### CHAPTER II

1 Quoted by Georges Bourgin, *L'État corporative en Italie*, Paris 1935, p.20.
2 Quoted by Gaudens Megaro, *Mussolini in the Making*, Boston and New York 1938, *passim*. Reproduced with the permission of the publishers, Messrs. Houghton, Mifflin Company.
3 Ibid., p.131.
4 Ibid., p. 327.
5 Speech of 25 November 1914.
6 *Popolo d'Italia*, 8 August 1919.
7 Quoted by A.Rossi, *La Naissance du Fascisme: De 1918 à 1922*, Paris 1938, p.23.
8 Speech of 19 March 1919.
9 *Popolo d'Italia*, 8 August 1919.
10 Ibid., 28 September 1920.
11 Ibid., 23 July 1919.
12 Ibid., 6 April 1920.
13 Quoted by Rossi, op. cit., p.113.
14 *Corriere della Sera*, 6 September 1920.
15 Quoted by Ignazio Silone, *Der Fascismus*, Zürich 1934, p.108.
16 In Proclamation of the Fascist Quadrumvirate, 29 October 1922. Quoted by Herbert W. Schneider, *Making the Fascist State*, New York 1928, p.392.
17 Gioacchino Volpe, *Lo sviluppo storico del Fascismo*, Palermo 1928, p.17.
18 Giacomo Matteotti (certainly no coward!) in a speech before the Chamber of Deputies, 10 March 1921. Quoted by Rossi, op. cit., p.90.
19 *Battaglie Sindacale*, 29 January 1921.
20 Quoted by Herman Finer, *Mussolini's Italy*, London 1935, p.151.
21 Quoted by Rossi, op. cit., p.201.

22 *L'Organizzazione Industriale*, 1 November 1922. Quoted by William Elwin, *Fascism at Work*, London 1934, p.46.

## CHAPTER III

1 Aristotle, *Politics*, Jowett translation, London 1923, Book V, c.11, pp.225–8.
2 Speech of 16 November 1922.
3 In *La Dottrina del Fascismo*, Milan 1935, p.38.
4 Statement made in March 1923.
5 Speech of 18 March 1923. Similarly, in his speech of 20 September 1922: 'It is necessary to end the railway state, the postal state, the insurance state.'
6 *Popolo di Lombardia*, 13 January 1923.
7 *L'Assalto* (Bologna), 14 April 1923.
8 Edoardo Frosini. Quoted by Silone, op. cit., p.170.
9 Circular letter to the provincial prefects. Quoted by Boris Schoenfeldt in Horace Taylor, *Contemporary Problems in the United States*, New York 1935, Vol.II, p.375.
10 Luigi Villari, 'The Economics of Fascism,' in G.S.Counts *et al.*, *Bolshevism, Fascism, and Capitalism*, New Haven 1932, p.204.
11 It is estimated that, during the years 1927–38, some 3,000 persons charged with political offenses were sentenced by the Special Tribunal to a total of 30,000 years' imprisonment; 4,600 persons were interned on penal islands and in other places of confinement; 12,700 were placed under police surveillance; 40,000 were warned not to interest themselves in politics; 280,000 were declared to be 'political suspects.'
12 Mario Missiroli, *What Italy Owes to Mussolini*, Rome 1937, p.34.
13 In 1937 the labor syndicates included about 78 per cent of the eligible employees; the employers' syndicates, about 50 per cent of the eligible employers.
14 Speech of 7 April 1926.
15 Speech of 21 April 1930.
16 Deputy Lusignoli in a speech before the Chamber of Deputies, 24 February 1932.
17 Speech of 14 November 1933.
18 There were eight Corporations relating to all stages of production, processing, and marketing of agricultural commodities (cereals; fruits, vegetables, and flowers; grapes and wine; beets and sugar; olives and olive oil; animal husbandry and fishing; forestry, lumber, and wood products; textile fibers and products); eight Corporations relating to the production and marketing of non-agricultural commodities (metallurgy and machinery; chemicals; clothing; paper and printing; building and public works; water, gas, and electricity; mining; glass and ceramics); and six Corporations relating to the production of services (sea and air transport; internal communications; the stage; tourism; insurance and credit; professions and arts).
19 Mussolini in a speech to members of the Comité France-Italie,

September 1933. Quoted by Daniel Guérin, *Fascisme et grand capital*, Paris 1936, p.170.

20  G.Bottai, quoted by Bourgin, op. cit., p.73.
21  Daniel Guérin, *Fascime et grand capital*, Paris 1936, p.76.
22  *Mussolini: An Outlook on Life* (anonymous), Rome 19[?], p.4.
23  Odon Por, in *New Britain*, 17 January 1934.
24  Speech of 10 October 1928.
25  V.Campogrando, *L'Ordinamento dello Stato Italiano*, Turin 1928, p.6.
26  *New York Times*, 20 January 1938.
27  Speech of 13 May 1929.
28  Cardinal Schuster, in a message of 26 February 1937.
29  Letter to Michele Bianchi, 27 August 1921.
30  Speech of 20 September 1921.
31  Carlo Curcio, 'Die geistige Grundlagen der korporativen Ordnung in Italien,' *Zeitschrift für Politik*, Vol. 20, 1930–1, p.407.
32  G.Lowell Field, *The Syndical and Corporative Institutions of Italian Fascism*, New York 1938, p.39.
33  Mussolini, in *Fascism: Doctrine and Institutions*, Rome 1935, note 15.
34  Ibid., note 1. Yet Mussolini could also say: 'We do not believe in programs, in plans, in saints or apostles, above all we do not believe in happiness, in salvation, in the promised land' (in *Diuturna*, Milan 1930).
35  *Mussolini: An Outlook on Life*, op. cit., p.8.

CHAPTER IV

1   Interview in *Paris-Soir*, 8 February 1928.
2   Speech of 6 October 1934.
3   Statement of 1 March 1926.
4   Silone, op. cit., p.203.
5   Field, op. cit., p.90.
6   *Lavoro Fascista*, 21 February 1931.
7   *Lavoro d'Italia*, 15 January 1929.
8   A.P.Dennis, in *World's Work*, August 1929, p.48.
9   *Corriere della Sera*, 26 March 1932.
10  G.Bottai, at one time Under-Secretary of Corporations, in *Il Sole*, 1 January 1931.
11  These observations on real wages are based on study of wage rates as fixed in labor contracts, on testimony of Fascist officials and the Fascist labor press, and on detailed analyses by economists. To be sure, certain official indexes of wages and costs of living show a slight rise in real wages after 1927. But they do not concur with underlying evidence.
12  *Lavoro Fascista*, 21 May 1929; *Lavoro Agricolo Fascista*, 7 August 1932, 31 July 1932.
13  *Lavoro Agricolo Fascista*, 7 August 1932.
14  Speech of 7 May 1928.
15  Speech of 20 September 1922.
16  Corrado Gini, at one time director of the Istituto Centrale di Statis-

tica, in C.E.McGuire, *Italy's International Economic Position*, New York 1927, p.515.

17  Deputy Zingali, in a speech before the Chamber of Deputies, 5 December 1929.

18  *Lavoro Fascista*, 8 October 1937.

19  L.Messedaglia, 'L'alimentazione dei contadini e la pellagra nel Veronese . . .,' *Atti dell'Accademia di agricoltura, scienze e lettere di Verona*, Serie V, VOL.VII, Verona 1930, p.360.

20  *Mussolini: An Outlook on Life*, op. cit., p.11.

21  Speech of 18 December 1930.

22  Istituto Centrale di Statistica, *Indagine sulle case rurali in Italia*, Rome 1934, p.7.

23  Giovanni Gerbino, *Ricostruzione corporativa*, Palermo 1937.

24  Quoted by Guérin, op. cit., p.151.

25  Arrigo Serpieri, at one time Under-Secretary for Land Reclamation, in *La legge sulla bonifica integrale nel primo anno di applicazione*, Rome 1931, pp.229–30.

26  Luigi Razza, at one time Minister of Public Works, in 'Convegno per la bonifica integrale . . .,' *Atti della R. Accademia dei Georgofili*, July–September 1934, p.358.

27  *Lavoro Agricolo Fascista*, 21 May 1929.

28  Ministry of Corporations, *News Notes on Fascist Corporations*, September 1932.

29  G.Tassinari, *Fascist Economy*, Rome 1937, p.23.

### Chapter V

1  Mussolini, *L'agricoltura e i rurali: Discorsi e scritti*, Rome 1931, pp.87, 109–10; A.Serpieri and N.Mazzocchi-Alemanni, *Lo Stato fascista e i rurali*, Milan 1935, *passim*.

2  G.Tassinari, Under-Secretary of Agriculture, in op. cit., p.102.

3  Speech of 28 October 1928.

4  Speech of 30 October 1926.

5  Franco Angelini, President of the Agricultural-Workers' Confederation, in *Lavoro Fascista*, 15 May 1937.

6  Edmondo Rossoni, quoted in *New Statesman and Nation*, 4 January 1936.

7  G.C.Baravelli, *La Bonification intégrale en Italie*, Rome 1935.

### Chapter VI

1  Speech of 18 March 1923.

2  Speech of 13 January 1934.

3  Speech of 6 October 1934.

4  Speech of 25 October 1924.

5  F.Ercole, *Dal Nazionalismo al Fascismo*, Rome 1928, p.62. Quoted by Elwin, op. cit., p.195.

6  Paul Einzig, *The Economic Foundations of Fascism*, London 1933, p.31.

7  Speech of 13 January 1934.

8  A.De'Stefani, speech of 25 November 1922.

9 Giacomo Acerbo, in a speech before the Chamber of Deputies, 12 December 1934.
10 Luigi Razza, in 'Convegno . . .,' op. cit., p.385.
11 Luigi Razza, ibid., pp.366–7.
12 Speech of 26 May 1934.
13 Speech of 15 October 1934.
14 In *L'Organisation corporative de l'État*, Rome 1929.
15 Speech of 23 March 1936.
16 Speech of 14 November 1933.
17 Speech of 8 November 1933.
18 *Popolo d'Italia*, 18 April 1933.
19 Speech of 15 May 1937.
20 Field, op. cit., p.202.
21 L.Rosenstock-Franck, *L'Économie corporative fasciste en doctrine et en fait*, Paris 1934, p.392.
22 A writer in *The Economist* (London) 27 July 1935.
23 Speech of 26 May 1934.
24 Speech of 10 November 1934.

### CHAPTER VII

1 Fascist Confederation of Industrialists, *Fascist Era: Year XV*, Rome 1937, p.94.
2 Speech of 23 March 1936.
3 Speech of 11 March 1936.
4 Speech of 26 May 1934.
5 Thaon de Revel, Minister of Finance, in a speech before the Chamber of Deputies, 18 May 1938.
6 Ibid.
7 *Corriere della Sera*, 26 January 1938.
8 Speech before the Chamber of Deputies, 5 March 1935.
9 Quoted by Harold Callender, *New York Times*, 18 July 1937.
10 Speech before the Chamber of Deputies, 23 March 1938.
11 Speech of 28 October 1937.
12 Ministry of Corporations, *News Notes on Fascist Corporations*, October 1937, p.8.
13 Speech of 24 September 1938, at Belluno.
14 G.Dallari, in Confederation Fasciste des Travailleurs de l'Agriculture, *La Charte du Travail et l'agriculture*, Rome 1937, p.126.
15 Mussolini, in speech of 26 May 1934.
16 Speech of 14 November 1933.
17 Mussolini, *Message for the Year IX*, 27 October 1930.
18 Thorstein Veblen, *The Theory of Business Enterprise*, New York 1904, pp.391–5, 398–400. Quoted with the permission of the publishers, Messrs. Charles Scribner's Sons.

# SELECTED BIBLIOGRAPHY

THIS list presents certain of the more useful and authoritative works on Italian Fascism. Obviously it makes no pretense to completeness.

Ascoli, Max, and Arthur Feiler: *Fascism For Whom?* New York, 1938. Includes an important study of the development and meaning of Italian Fascism.

Biagi, Bruno: *Lo Stato corporativo*. Rome, 1934. An official statement.

Borgese, G.A.: *Goliath: The March of Fascism*. New York, 1937. An 'emotional' interpretation of Fascism. Brilliant exposition.

Bottai, G.: *Le Corporazioni*. Milan, 1935. An official statement.

Bourgin, Georges: *L'État corporative en Italie*. Paris, 1935. A brief history.

Dobbert, Gerhard (ed.): *Die faschistische Wirtschaft*. Berlin, 1934. A collection of articles by a number of scholars and officials, chiefly German and Italian, on various aspects of the Italian economy.

Einzig, Paul: *The Economic Foundations of Fascism*. London, 1933. Sympathetic with Fascism.

Elwin, William: *Fascism at Work*. London, 1934. Anti-Fascist.

Field, G. Lowell: *The Syndical and Corporative Institutions of Italian Fascism*. New York, 1938. A scholarly study of the structure of the Corporate State.

Finer, Herman: *Mussolini's Italy*. London, 1935. Very informative, especially on the politics of Fascism.

Guérin, Daniel: *Fascisme et grand capital*. Paris, 1936. Anti-Fascist.

Haider, Carmen: *Capital and Labor under Fascism*. New York, 1930. Scholarly, critical.

Istituto Centrale di Statistica del Regno d'Italia: *Annuario Statistico Italiano.* Rome, annually. Indispensable statistics.

Macartney, Maxwell H.H., and Paul Cremona: *Italy's Foreign and Colonial Policy, 1914–1937.* London and New York, 1938. Very informative.

McGuire, C.E.: *Italy's International Economic Position.* New York, 1927. An informative description of the Italian economy in the early 1920's.

Megaro, Gaudens: *Mussolini in the Making.* New York and Boston, 1938. A revealing study of Mussolini before the World War.

Michels, Roberto: *Italien von Heute.* Leipzig, 1930. Sympathetic with Fascism.

Mortara, Giorgio: *Prospettive economiche.* Cittá di Castello, 1922–6; Milan, 1926 ff. Valuable economic annals.

Mussolini, Benito: *Scritti e discorsi.* Milan, 1934 ff. The official edition of the Duce's speeches.

——*Fascism: Doctrine and Institutions.* Rome, 1935. The authoritative statement.

——*The Corporate State.* Florence, 1936. Speeches, documents, and bibliography.

Perroux, F.: *Contribution a l'étude de l'économie et des finances publiques de l'Italie depuis la guerre.* Paris, 1929. Informative.

Pitigliani, Fausto: *The Corporative State.* New York, 1934. A pro-Fascist study of formal structure.

Rosenstock-Franck, L.: *L'Économie corporative fasciste en doctrine et en fait.* Paris, 1934. Scholarly, critical. A valuable study of Fascism-in-action.

Rossi, A.: *La Naissance du Fascisme: De 1918 à 1922.* Paris, 1938. An outstanding history of early Fascism. Highly critical.

Salvemini, Gaetano: *The Fascist Dictatorship in Italy.* New York, 1927. A history of Fascism's rise to power.

——*Under the Axe of Fascism.* New York, 1936. An analysis of labor and capital under the Dictatorship. These highly critical books, together with the author's periodical articles, are indispensable to an understanding of Fascism.

Sarfatti, M.: *The Life of Benito Mussolini.* New York, 1925. A eulogy.

Schmidt, Carl T.: *The Plough and the Sword: Labor, Land, and Property in Fascist Italy.* New York, 1938. A critical study of agriculture under Fascism. Bibliography.

Schneider, Herbert W.: *Making the Fascist State.* New York, 1928. A detailed account of Fascism's rise to power. Bibliography.

Schneider, Herbert W., and S.B.Clough: *Making Fascists.* Chicago, 1929. A study of educational and propaganda processes.

Seldes, George: *Sawdust Caesar.* New York, 1935. An unflattering portrait of Mussolini.

Silone, Ignazio: *Der Fascismus.* Zürich, 1934. An anti-Fascist interpretation, especially interesting for its analysis of the immediate background of Fascism. See also Silone's remarkable novels, *Fontamara* (New York, 1934) and *Bread and Wine* (New York, 1937), for description of life under Fascist rule.

Spencer, H.R.: *Government and Politics of Italy.* Yonkers, N.Y., 1932. A useful brief account.

Spirito, Ugo: *I fondamenti dell'economia corporativa.* Milan, 1932. An interpretation by a 'collectivist' Fascist.

Steiner, H. Arthur: *Government in Fascist Italy.* New York, 1938. An informative, concise study of formal political institutions. Bibliography.

Vöchting, Friedrich: *Die Romagna: Eine Studie über Halbpacht und Landarbeiterwesen in Italien.* Karlsruhe, 1927.

——*Die Urbarmachung der römischen Campagna.* Zürich, 1935. Although these are detailed studies of social and economic problems of particular localities, they throw penetrating light on the character of Fascism.

Volpe, Gioacchino: *Lo Sviluppo storico del Fascismo.* Palermo, 1928. An official history.

Welk, William G.: *Fascist Economic Policy.* Cambridge, Mass., 1938. Contains valuable economic data. Bibliography.

# INDEX

ABYSSINIA, colonization of, 139–40
Abyssinian war, 81, 85, 137ff., 145
Agricultural policy, Fascist, 97–8
Agricultural workers, 6, 17, 27, 80, 82, 94–6, 98, 103, 112
Agriculture,
under the old regime, 5–7, 11–12
under Fascism, 97ff.
*Ansaldo*, 21
Anti-semitism, 155
Aosta, Duke of, 47
Arias, Gino, 132
Aristotle on tyranny, 49
Armament economy, 140ff.
Armaments, 11, 12, 143, 144
*Avanti!*, 37

BADOGLIO, Pietro, 47
Banks and banking, 11, 123ff., 143
Barter agreements, 126
Battle of Wheat, 98–105, 141
Benni, Antonio Stefano, 94
Biagi, Bruno, 80
Blackshirt Militia, 51, 61
*Bonifica integrale, see* Land reclamation
Bottai, Giuseppe, 131
Bread, 97, 103–4, 147, 152
*Breda*, 21, 151n.
Brenner Pass, 154
Bureaucracy, its growing powers, 116, 120, 129ff., 151ff.

CAPITAL levies, 145, 151
Cartelization of industry, 21, 120ff.
Catholic church, under Fascism, 71–2

Catholic labor unions, 15, 27, 44
Catholic Populist Party, 22–3, 28, 30–1, 39, 54, 55
Central Corporative Committee, 66, 143, 152
Chamber of Deputies, 8, 59–60
Chamber of Fasces and Corporations, 60
Charter of Labor, 67–8, 75, 79–80, 115
Charter of Share-Tenancy, 112
Class-collaboration, 15, 28, 52, 56, 75, 79, 159
Collective labor contracts, 29, 78
Colonization, 84, 110, 140
Communist Party, 45
Concentration, industrial and financial, 120ff.
Confederations, syndical, 63
Co-operatives, 16, 25, 28, 31, 44
Corporate 'philosophy,' 67–9, 92, 132
Corporate system, 62ff., 115ff.
Corporations, Fascist, 62, 66–7, 131–4
*Corriere della Sera*, 40
Cost of living, 26, 81
Courts of Labor, 64, 93–4
Cultural decadence, 154ff.

D'ANNUNZIO, Gabriele, 22, 33, 72
Death rates, 89
Depression, economic, 24–5, 119ff.
'Deproletarization,' 94–6, 112
Discontent, popular, 149, 152–3
*Dopolavoro*, 86, 88
Duce, *see* Mussolini

EDUCATION, 70–1, 89, 155
Election of 1919, 22, 26, 27, 28, 39
  of 1921, 45
  of 1924, 54
Electoral law of 1924, 54
Emigrant remittances, 16, 84, 120
Emigration, 15–16, 84, 110, 114,
  139, 148
Employment, 85–6
Enclosures, 113
Ethiopia, *see* Abyssinia
Expropriation of Jews, 145
Expropriation of landlords, 98,
  107, 110

FAILURES, business, 120, 130
Fasci di combattimento, 34, 43
*Fascio di Azione rivoluzionaria*,
  34
Fascist employers' associations,
  63–5, 76
Fascist Grand Council, 58, 59, 60
Fascist labor unions, 63–5, 76ff.
Fascist movement, early,
  beginnings, 34ff.
  program, 38–9
  serves reaction, 40ff.
  growth, 41ff.
  aided by Government, 43, 45
  attacks labor unions, 43–4
  seizure of power, 47ff.
Fascist Party,
  founding, 43
  internal dissensions, 52–3
  character, 58–9
Fascist regime,
  early policies, 50ff.
  establishment of dictatorship,
    55ff.
  its development, 56ff., 143ff.
*Fiat*, 21, 150, 151n.
Finances, governmental, 25–6,
  46, 127–9, 144–6
Fiume, 22, 33
Food consumption, 90–1, 104
Foreign trade, 17, 117ff., 125–7,
  138, 147
Forty-hour week, 84
Freemasons, 56

Fruit and vegetable production,
  101, 103
Futurists, 18, 35

GENERAL Confederation of
  Agriculture, 40
General Confederation of
  Industry, 40, 47, 63, 94, 121
General Confederation of Labor,
  15, 26, 27, 51
Gold reserves, 126, 147n.
Grand Council of Fascism, 58,
  59, 60
Guarneri, Felice, 148, 150

HOURS of work, 13, 29, 82, 84
Housing conditions, 91–2

*Ilva*, 21
Industrial concentration, 20,
  120ff.
Industrial financing, 122ff., 143
Industrial workers, 13, 29, 80ff.
Industrialists, and Fascism, 40,
  46–8, 54, 62–3, 115–16,
  149–51
Industrialization of Italy, 10ff.,
  116ff.
Intellectuals,
  and the old regime, 10, 18
  and Fascism, 154–5

JOURNALISM, 56, 69–70

LABOR Charter, 67–8, 75, 79–
  80, 115
Labor courts, 64, 93–4
Labor disputes, 64, 93–4
Labor movement,
  rise, 14ff.
  in post-war period, 26ff.
  under Fascism, 75ff.
Land reclamation, 105–11
Land tenure, 6, 111–13
Landlords, and Fascism, 40, 41,
  43, 46, 51, 98, 103, 104, 106–
  7, 109ff., 127, 130, 134
*Lanital*, 142
Lateran Treaty, 71

*Latifondi*, 6, 30, 98
League of Nations, 28, 137
Leo XIII, 15
*Libretto di lavoro*, 79n.
Lion of Judah, 152
Lira devaluation, 147
Lira stabilization, 118–19
Livestock industry, 101–2, 111
Living standards, 5, 7, 16, 89ff., 149, 152, 158
Local government, 60–1
Lockouts, forbidden, 64, 79

MACHIAVELLI, Nicolò, 35, 72
March on Rome, 47
Matteotti, Giacomo, 55
Matteotti crisis, 55–6
Middle classes, under Fascism, 41, 42, 58, 77, 128, 130, 131, 149, 152ff., 158–9
Ministry of Corporations, 64, 77, 78, 93, 96, 121, 152
Ministry of Propaganda, 69
*Montecatini*, 21, 122, 150, 151n.
Morgan loan, 117n.
Mussolini, Benito,
    character, 35–7, 153
    deserts Socialism, 37
    champion of the workers, 35–8
    leader of Fascist movement, 34, 38ff.
    becomes Prime Minister, 47, 50
    criticized by early followers, 52–3
    becomes dictator, 55
    his powers, 57ff.
    deification, 73, 153–4
    harvests wheat, 97
    drains Pontine Marshes, 109
    his popularity, 153
Mussolini, Benito,
    on agriculture, 97
    on autarchy, 141
    on the bourgeoisie, 39
    on capital and labor, 75, 115
    on capitalism, 115, 151–2, 156
    on Catholicism, 71
    on corporate economy, 64, 115, 156

on Corporations, 65–6, 131–3, 135, 156
on diet, 91
on economic depression, 119, 135
on Fascist 'philosophy,' 72–3, 156
on Fascist purposes, 38, 39, 40, 46, 50, 52, 64, 65–6, 76, 116, 141
on Fascist syndicates, 76
on 'guns or butter,' 153
on 'higher social justice,' 76
on housing, 92
on journalism, 70
on labor, 38, 75–6, 115
on labor courts, 94
on land reclamation, 105, 106
on his 'mania,' 37
on matter and spirit, 74
on militarism, 36
on National Council of Corporations, 65
on nationalism, 35
on the occupation of the factories, 1920, 38
on police persecution, 36
on private property, 115
on profiteers, 38
on provincial government, 61
on refinancing institutions, 125
on small business, 131
on social legislation, 86, 89
on stabilization of the lira, 118
on the State, 35, 39, 50, 52, 73
on the strike, 38
on taxation policy, 144, 151
on war, 141, 155
Mussolini, Vittorio, 156

NAPOLEON, 4
National Council of Corporations, 65, 124n.
National debt, 129, 146
Nationalism, 10, 18, 33, 48, 154
Nationalist Party, 18, 35, 42, 53, 71
Newspapers, 55, 56, 69–70
Nietzsche, Friedrich, 35, 72

OCCUPATION of factories, 1920, 31–3
*Opera Nazionale Combattenti*, 108

PAPACY,
and the old regime, 9
and Fascism, 71–2
Pareto, Vilfredo, 35, 72
Parliamentary regime, 8–9, 33, 51, 59–60
*Passo romano*, 154
Peasants, 5–8, 15–16, 20, 26, 29–30, 41, 95, 97ff., 112, 152
Penal code, 61–2
Pirelli, 131
Pius XI, 71
Podestà, 61
Police controls, 61–2
Political organization of Fascism, 55ff.
Politics under the old regime, 8–9
Pontine Marshes, 108–9
*Popolo d'Italia*, 37, 132
Populists, *see* Catholic Populist Party
Post-war conditions, economic and political, 25ff.
Praetorian Guard, 156
Press, under Fascism, 69–70
Price control, 100, 143, 147
Profits, business, 21, 26, 39, 51, 118, 119, 120, 139, 150–1, 158
Propaganda, Fascist, 69, 72, 153–4
Provincial Councils of Corporations, 64–5
Public debt, *see* National debt
Public health, 89
Public works, 85

RATIONALIZATION, industrial, 21, 120–1
Reclamation, *see* Land reclamation
*Rerum novarum*, 15
*Risorgimento*, 4–5, 10, 19
Romanism, Fascist, 73

Rossoni, Edmondo, 42, 63n., 77, 112, 141, 149
Rural population, 5–6, 112
Russian Revolution, 26

SANCTIONS, League of Nations', 1935–6, 137–8
Self-sufficiency, economic, 98, 99, 100, 104, 140ff.
Senate, 60
Share-cropping, 84, 95–6, 98, 111
Share-tenancy, 6, 98, 103, 112
*Snia Viscosa*, 151 n.
Social insurance, 17, 28–9, 83, 86–8
Social legislation, 17, 28–9, 86–9
Social structure under the old regime, 5–8
Socialism, 13, 14, 15, 17, 31, 33, 35, 42, 68, 115, 156
Socialist Party, 15, 19, 22–3, 27–8, 30–3, 36, 37, 45, 51, 55
Sorel, Georges, 35, 72
South Italy, 7–8, 12–13, 43n., 102–3
Spanish Civil War, 145, 152
Stabilization of the lira, 80, 118–19
Standard of living, 86ff., 149
Strikes (1919–20), 29, 32–3
Strikes, prohibited, 64, 79
Strikes, under Fascism, 79
Subsidization of business, 11–12, 21, 25, 123–5, 127, 128, 130–1, 150
Syndicalism, 15
Syndicalist unions, 15, 27, 42
Syndicate officials, 76–8, 94
Syndicates, Fascist, 63–4, 75–9, 94

TARIFFS, protective, 4, 8, 11, 100, 103, 104, 105, 114, 117, 126
'Tax in workers,' 84
Taxation policy, 51, 127–9, 144–6
*Terni*, 150
Terrorism, Fascist, 43–4, 45, 46, 55–6, 62

Tourism, 26, 120, 126, 147n., 148
Trade unions, *see* Labor movement
Tripolitan War, 19, 35
Tuberculosis insurance, 86, 87

UNEMPLOYMENT, 82–6, 135, 138
Unemployment insurance, 83, 86, 87
Unemployment relief, 83–6, 109
Urbanism, 97–8

VEBLEN, Thorstein, 157
Victor Emmanuel III, 47, 60

Violations of labor contracts, 82, 93–4
Volpe, G., 43

WAGES, under the old regime, 13, 17, 29
under Fascism, 79–83, 123
Wheat, 6, 98–105, 147
Working hours, 13, 17, 29, 82, 84
World War, Italy's participation, 19–22
its social and economic consequences, 20–6

YOUTH, under Fascism, 70–1, 74, 89, 155–6